Rooted Deep in the Pigeon Valley

A Harvest of Western Carolina Memories

To Ed and Ronnie with
Kindest Regards!
Carroll C. Jones

Also by Carroll C. Jones

The 25th North Carolina Troops in the Civil War: History and Roster of a Mountain-Bred Regiment

Rooted Deep in the Pigeon Valley

A Harvest of Western Carolina Memories

Carroll C. Jones

FOREWORD BY EDIE HUTCHINS BURNETTE

PUBLISHED BY WINOCA PRESS
P. O. Box 30, Wilmington, NC 28402-0300 USA • www.winocapress.com

Available direct from the publisher, from your local bookstore, or from the author at cjhargrove@bellsouth.com

Printed in the United States of America
12 11 10 09 5 4 3 2 1

LIBRARY OF CONGRESS CATALOGING-IN-PUBLICATION DATA
Jones, Carroll C.
Rooted deep in the Pigeon Valley : a harvest of Western Carolina memories / Carroll C. Jones ; foreword by Edie Hutchins Burnette.
p. cm.
Includes bibliographical references.
ISBN 978-0-9789736-4-3 (cloth)
ISBN 978-0-9789736-5-0 (trade paper)
1. Haywood County (N.C.)—History, Local—Anecdotes. I. Title.
F262.H35J66 2009
975.6′94—dc22 2009017167

Book cover and interior designed by Barbara Brannon
Cover illustration by Mary Jo Owen; used by permission
Title page: Pigeon Valley homestead, circa 1950s; photograph by Albert C. (Tony) Jones. Collection of the author.

To Rego, who shares
my feelings about our Pigeon
Valley heritage, and to the
memory of our parents,
Tony and Jimmie Hargrove Jones

Contents

Illustrations and Maps

ILLUSTRATIONS *continued*

Foreword

CARROLL JONES HAS WRITTEN an informative and entertaining collection of stories that provide insight into the lives of the hardy pioneers who settled in the rich and beautiful area of North Carolina called Pigeon Valley. Vivid imagery echoes memories etched in his mind of times he spent in the 1950s and '60s in this verdant valley and surrounding area. The pages of this book make a good read for both those familiar with this area as well as those who are not.

The author and I share many things, including great-grandfather William "Hack" Hargrove and great-great-great-great-grandfather Jacob Shook. His grandmother, Margaret Haseltine Shook Evans Hargrove, was Aunt Mag to me, although she was actually sister to Mary Shook Hargrove, my grandmother. His grandfather James Hargrove was brother to my grandfather Joe Hargrove. Thus, Carroll and I are double second cousins and belong to the fifth generation of Hargroves descended from William Manson Hartgrove, who first settled along the upper reaches of Haywood County's Pigeon River in the early 1820s.

Raised on neighboring farms in the Pigeon Valley during the Depression years, his mother and her three sisters and my mother and her three sisters were thick as thieves. They were all fiercely proud of their Hargrove heritage. With diverse personalities, they might disagree among themselves—but beware to any person who might harm any one of the six with words or deeds, for they would be confronted with a united, spirited defense.

Beyond these common bloodlines, Carroll and I also share treasure troves of memories of youthful and adult years spent at our grandparents' neighboring houses. We both roamed the mountains backdropping the homeplaces, swam in the cold, clear Pigeon River, participated to a limited degree in the farm work, enjoyed gatherings centered around such things as molasses cookoffs or cider renderings. We are both smitten with a deep, abiding love for our area of Pigeon Valley and the thirst to glean information, both important and trivial, about our shared heritage and record it, he in books and I in weekly columns for the *Asheville Citizen-Times' Haywood County News.*

Carroll has succeeded in capturing much of the essence of those early settlers in Pigeon Valley with masterful assemblages of words and sentences. He has supplemented his lucid memories with extensive research in order to provide accurate and colorful pictures of early life in the Valley, as well as the travails and opportunities created by the years of the Civil War and its aftermath. He has moved forward in time as well to describe growing-up years in the town of Canton in Haywood County, North Carolina, located just a short distance down river from the historic Pigeon Valley area.

The influences that shaped Carroll in his passage from child to adulthood as part of the Hargrove clan have served him well. He was an outstanding athlete in his youth, and his obvious intelligence, his education, and his upbringing have carried him through a successful professional career and the roles of loving son, brother, husband, and father to two girls. Although he no longer dwells in North Carolina, I suspect that a large portion of his heart and soul makes its forever home in Pigeon Valley.

A retired employee of International Paper Company, formerly Champion International, Carroll is currently working as an engineering consultant in Pensacola, Florida. In his precious spare time he busies himself, as can be seen, recapturing in words the history of a long-ago time for both his and our enjoyment. He has published a previous book, *The 25th North Carolina Troops in the Civil War: History and Roster of a Mountain-Bred Regiment,* inspired by his desire and quest to learn of his great-grandfather Captain Hack Hargrove's service to the Confederacy.

Carroll's literary work to date has not only unveiled the rich history of the region but also has clearly demonstrated his rightful claim of being deeply rooted in the Pigeon Valley.

EDITH CAROLYN (EDIE) HUTCHINS BURNETTE
Canton, North Carolina

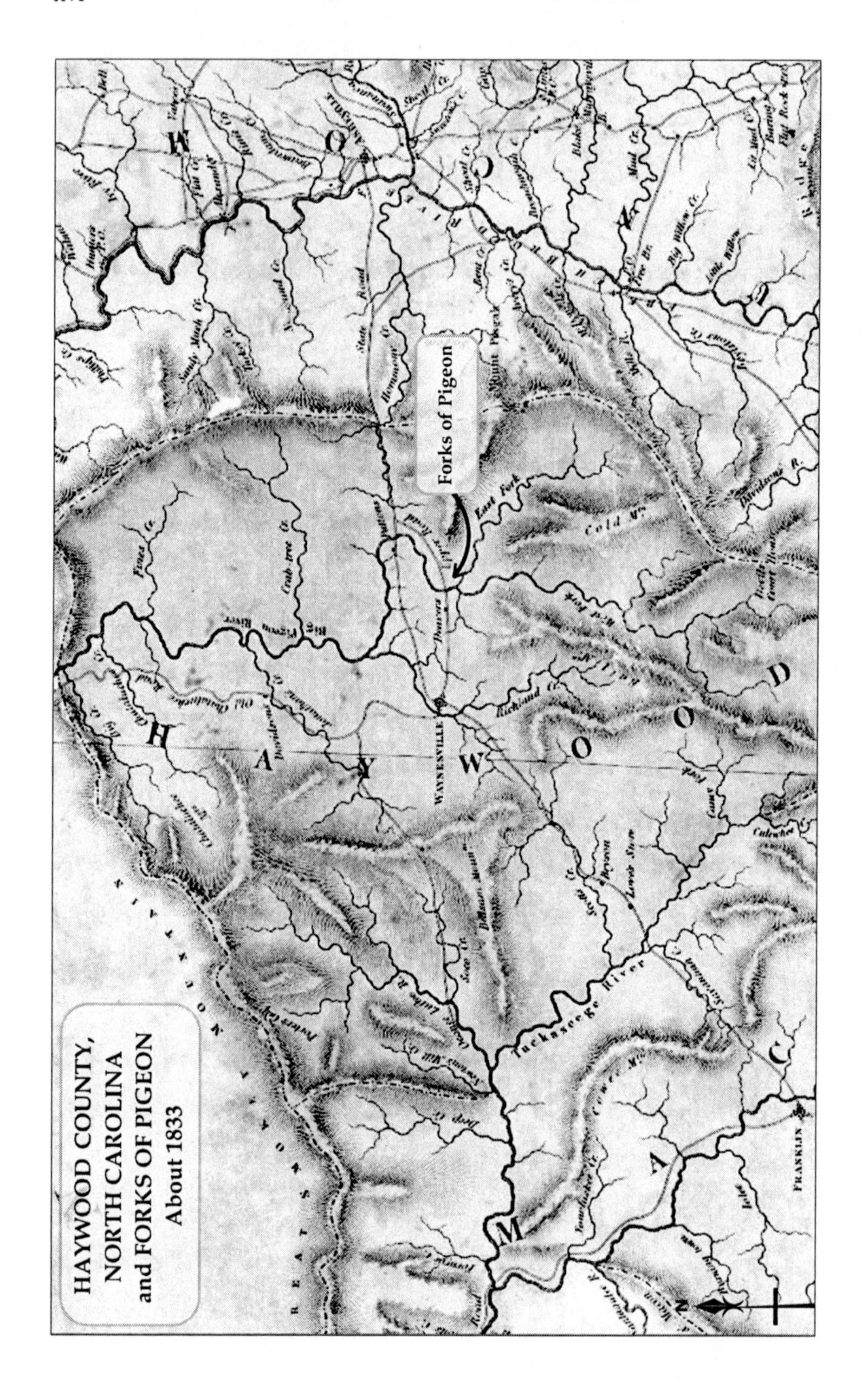
HAYWOOD COUNTY,
NORTH CAROLINA
and FORKS OF PIGEON
About 1833
Forks of Pigeon
WAYNESVILLE
FRANKLIN
Big Pigeon River
Tuckaseege River
East Fork
Cold Mtn
Richland Cr.
Davidson's R.
State Road
H A Y W O O D
Crab-tree Cr.

A Note from the Author

A FEW YEARS AGO, AFTER RETIRING from a thirty-plus-year career in the paper industry, I was beset with a gnawing, compelling urge to write about my rich heritage that was linked to the Pigeon Valley in Haywood County, North Carolina. After all, my great-grandfather was a Civil War veteran, county politician, and state legislator and was hailed as Canton's "first citizen" by his contemporaries.

And, too, my maternal grandfather up and vacated the Pigeon Valley as a young man for reasons that still escape us today. He apparently was so consumed by an adventurous spirit and infected with a fever for gold so strong that he spent more than twenty years in search of that precious metal. After tramping around in the Old West boom towns that had sprung up in Montana, Nevada, and California he finally returned to the Pigeon Valley for good. And with him he brought back a jar of gold dust that still gleams brightly in his grandson's mind. I set out on a quest to find and follow the faint footsteps of these grand ancestors of mine to whatever haunts they might lead. To some degree I was successful in tracking them down, and inside these pages the reader will become acquainted with "Captain" William Harrison Hargrove and his son, James Burton Hargrove.

Additionally, I offer a description of the Pigeon Valley that both these men called home. From the time that the first hardy and courageous pioneers broke though the mountain ramparts to settle the lands straddling the upper Pigeon River, the area known then as Forks of Pigeon has been one of the most productive and prosperous in Haywood County. Hargroves, Catheys, and Moores were among those early settlers and the pages of this book reveal my ties to these families and just how I came to be so deeply rooted to the Pigeon Valley.

I must admit, however, that I am not a Pigeon Valley native myself, strictly speaking. You see, I'm a city boy, having been born and raised in the mill town of Canton about four miles down the river. During the 1950s and '60s when I was growing up in that fair city there were probably about five thousand inhabitants, and I surely came to know most of them. The reader will find enclosed herein a brief description of my hometown and the memories that are sometimes provoked when I reflect back on blissful childhood days in Canton.

Although Canton is removed by some several miles' distance from the site of the early Forks of Pigeon settlement, it was close enough to my grandmother's farm, located smack in the middle of the Pigeon Valley, that we were able to visit with her frequently. I have vivid memories of countless trips up the "backside" of the river to Granny Hargrove's house. So great an impression did these excursions to "the country" make on me that I have tried to capture their essence in an account titled "Granny Hargrove's House." It is my hope that the reader will be swept along on this fanciful diversion and share the joys and delights of an adolescent privileged to experience the rural setting and trappings of his mountain farming heritage.

The balance of this anthology comprises a mixture of serious treatments of historical topics related to the Pigeon Valley and a couple of lighter matters that will provide the reader with a little hilarity and maybe even a chuckle or two. Thrown in for good measure, and seasoning, are the author's random musings about the distinct seasons of the year and how they influenced the lives and circumstances of the Pigeon Valley pioneers.

Readers of these accounts are advised to take their contemporary hats off for a spell and let imaginations run unbridled as they take a journey back in time. The tickets and conveyance for these transportations will be provided by the memories and histories and stories recorded within. Hunker down, relax, and enjoy the trip!

Rooted Deep in the Pigeon Valley

A Harvest of Western Carolina Memories

At the turn of the nineteenth century pioneer families like the one depicted here began settling the fertile lands along the upper Pigeon River. (Illustration by Elizabeth Cramer McClure from Ora Blackmun, *Western North Carolina, Its Mountains and Its People to 1880,* 1977; used by permission.)

Opposite: From Rebecca Harding Davis, "By-paths in the Mountains," *Harper's New Monthly Magazine* 61 (1880).

Prologue Forks of Pigeon in the Early Years

In the midst of the Blue Ridge Mountain Range, whose peaks protrude high into the sky over western North Carolina's Haywood County, a fertile valley lies astraddle the Pigeon River. The first pioneers reached the Pigeon Valley at the onset of the 1800s as the Cherokee Indians retreated further westward into the remotest reaches of the mountains, their migration forced upon them through treaty after treaty with the English colonies and most recently the fledgling government of the United States of America.[1] Those original brave settlers of primarily Scots-Irish, English and German descent claimed the rich bottomlands near the rivers. Others arriving later settled in the coves along smaller streams and creeks and higher up on the mountainsides and ridgetops.[2] A community of mostly farming homesteads rose up where the east and west tributaries of the Pigeon River are joined and became known as Forks of Pigeon.

In the early years before the river's power was harnessed by sawmills, the pioneers built small log cabins to live in. They used great

A cabin's hearth drew mountaineer families together. (From Rebecca Harding Davis, "By-paths in the Mountains," *Harper's New Monthly Magazine* 61 [1880]).

care in choosing building sites that were near a good source of water, well drained, and elevated so the flooding river and creek waters posed no hazard. From the surrounding forests these hardy men and women felled huge trees with axes and built the structures by stacking one log on top of another. The pioneer, wielding only an ax and adze to shape the logs, crafted the corner joints in an interlocking fashion to secure the logs in place. The most important element of the cabin, of course, was the fireplace, which was typically built of mountain stone or river rock collected nearby. These materials were laid up, often very crudely, and fixed together with a muddy mixture of clay and straw. Not only did the hearth keep the small cabin relatively warm during the cold winters, but it also provided the heat for cooking and a source of light for the dark cabin interior. Most of all,

Early settlers of the Forks of Pigeon region built crude log cabins and grew corn and wheat crops on their small mountain homesteads, as depicted in this whimsical sketch. (From Wilbur G. Zeigler and Ben S. Grosscup, *The Heart of the Alleghanies,* 1883.)

however, it served as a gathering place that welcomed the family to congregate and enjoy one another's company.

Farmers lucky enough to claim tracts of bottomland were rewarded with rich alluvial soil that was easily broken and readied for planting. Higher up on the mountainsides the settlers were not so fortunate. There the soil was rocky, less productive, and more difficult to work. No matter their lot, the Valley's pioneer farmers were a hardy and determined sort. They fretted little over hard work, and through tremendous toil and exertions caused the Pigeon Valley to bloom with their precious crops.

Each spring, along about March or April, the Valley gradually exchanged its dark gray shroud for a beautiful green veil infinitely spotted with colorful blossoms of the serviceberry, mountain laurel, rhododendron, and dogwood trees. It was in this picturesque setting, with the scent of wild onion and damp earth in the air, that the early settlers applied their energies to break the ground, using horses or mules to pull plows or by simply wielding hoes and crude digging tools. These exhaustive efforts were aimed toward raising corn and wheat crops to feed their families and livestock. Any surplus grain that might be realized was bartered for necessities that could not be produced at home such as salt, sugar, iron tools, cloth, medicine, and other goods. And it was not uncommon in the day for the farmers to trade their hard-won yields for the services of a doctor, hired hand, blacksmith, traveling cobbler, teacher, or even a preacher. Grain crops were in this way the Valley's treasure and the currency that fueled the region's economic engine.

In those early days the roads were important improvements that the Pigeon Valley settlers made to enhance the development of their community. Crops and goods had to be moved into, out of, and throughout the Valley to the mills and to markets. This was facilitated somewhat during dry weather by their existing crude roads, which the laws required able-bodied men to work on. Often, however, especially during the winter months, these roads were no more

Crude log cabins provided shelter for Pigeon Valley families for more than a century as settlers eked out a subsistence in the rugged mountain lands. (George Grantham Bain Collection, Library of Congress.)

than narrow traces of ruts and muddy washouts that offered little advantage to farmers opting to use them.

Just after the formation of Haywood County in 1808, the newly elected county officials ordered two wagon roads to be "marked out and made" to connect the Pigeon Valley with outside communities. One road ran from Waynesville across Pigeon Gap (along present-day Highway 276) into the East Fork area. Another, connecting the Beaverdam area (present-day Canton) with the Pigeon Valley, snaked along the Pigeon River passing John McDowell's "flowery garden" (or Garden Creek) and connected with the upper Pigeon road previously mentioned.[3] In addition, the Western Turnpike, completed sometime around 1850, was the primary umbilical between Asheville and Waynesville and points further west.[4] This critical road passed near where the town of Canton is located today and served the Pigeon Valley folk as the principal link to the Buncombe Turnpike and, thereby, the outside markets in Tennessee, South Carolina, and Georgia.

A mill and general store owned by "Colonel" Joseph Cathey was in operation in those early years near where the waters of the East Fork and West Fork rivers combine to create the Pigeon River. Cathey has been described as one of the most capable and influential men of his time in the county. His store was reportedly one of the largest and most successful around. It was stocked with a generous variety of supplies needed by the mostly self-sufficient farmers—goods and equipment that the farmers were not able to produce or craft for themselves. Integral to this mercantile business was the local post office, which occupied a small space within the store's walls and had the aptly named postal address of "Forks of Pigeon."[5]

Nearby, the Cathey gristmill, powered by its huge fourteen-foot diameter undershot wheel and water diverted from the river, groaned continuously as the farmers' hard-won harvests were ground between great granite millstones.[6] The commerce and facility provided by the store and mill made these Cathey enterprises the hub of the local community and economy. It was here that settlers brought their valuable corn and wheat crops to be milled into corn meal and flour, bought and traded for much-needed supplies, and communicated with each other and the outside world.

The blacksmiths provided another essential service to the Pigeon Valley farmers. They were powerful and skilled men with an extraordinary ability to heat, beat, weld, and shape iron over hot forges into useful implements and hardware. Their iron fabrications and repairs were necessary, of course, for the settlers to build and maintain productive homesteads—the underpinning of their community. During the early days in the Valley, brothers John and Alfred Franklin Hartgrove were local blacksmiths who plied their skills as a livelihood and were for a time attached to the Cathey enterprises on the grounds surrounding the store and mill.[7]

As the Pigeon Valley settlement grew, at least three different churches were organized in the Valley to provide for the spiritual needs and welfare of the people. Many of the hard-working pioneer families were devoted Christians and faithfully received religious and moral guidance at either the Baptist, Presbyterian, or Methodist church.[8] These churches, and their associated camp meetings, were main focal points of social activity and congregation during the early days in the Pigeon Valley. Camp meetings, usually held in the late summer, were always popular events. Entire families packed up their belongings and traveled to the meeting grounds where, along with their neighbors, they camped out and worshipped for entire weeks at a time. It was not uncommon for these epic religious revivals to be coordinated around the schedule of some renowned traveling minister or evangelist. In that case, full advantage could be taken of the singular oratory and spiritual gifts possessed by those dedicated and tireless preachers.[9]

In 1838 a fine two-room schoolhouse was constructed to serve the community on land donated by Elijah Deaver near where the present-day Bethel Middle School stands. It was a frame and board building, and anchoring each end were heavy brick fireplaces and chimneys. These masonry structures were built by William Manson Hartgrove from brick fashioned by his own hands. Along one side of the school building windows provided light and ventilation, and on the opposing side a door allowed access to the rustic learning institute.[10] In addition to this school, which was free to all students, subscription schools were not uncommon, and parents or guardians could "subscribe," or contract, with the teacher for their children's education. Not uncommonly, the teacher's fees would be bartered for bushels of corn or wheat, sides of meat, days of labor, and the like.

Life in the valley during those early times was surely difficult and filled with challenges and hardships not easily imagined today. However, residents of the Valley found diversions from their daily work that tended to lighten their spirits and provide sparks of enjoyment and fun to keep their hopes kindled. Womenfolk, for example, could derive satisfaction from their laborious and vital homespun work. Significant amounts of their time and toil were exerted in spinning wool, cotton, and flax into yarn and thread. These materials were in turn woven, sewn, and fashioned into artful and practical clothing and coverings for their families. Though tedious and demanding, this essential craft work surely provided enjoyment and pleasure to the pioneer women as well as prideful feelings for their creations.

Hunting, trapping, and fishing were, of course, vital pursuits of the menfolk which provided food for the table, clothing for the family, and furs to fend against the cold. But for the men and boys, these activities offered a welcome escape from their routine labors and diversions during the long winters. Additionally, the men were frequent visitors to Cathey's store and mill, where they could take delight in passing time with friends and catching up on the latest news, gossip, and tales.

Throughout the year there were plentiful opportunities for everyone—men, women, children, and young folk—to participate in community gatherings and activities. These proceedings provided excitement and a bit of gaiety and variety in their lives and included church gatherings and singings, corn huskings and hoedowns in the fall, quiltings for the women and girls, barn raisings, molasses-candy pulling in the winter, square dances and such.

Forks of Pigeon was not an extraordinary community, nor was it significantly different from others spread throughout the western North Carolina mountains. It was a typical rural mountain community that possessed the essential elements required for the citizens to work, worship, learn, and flourish. And in the very early days this Pigeon Valley settlement developed into one of the most prosperous and progressive population centers in Haywood County.

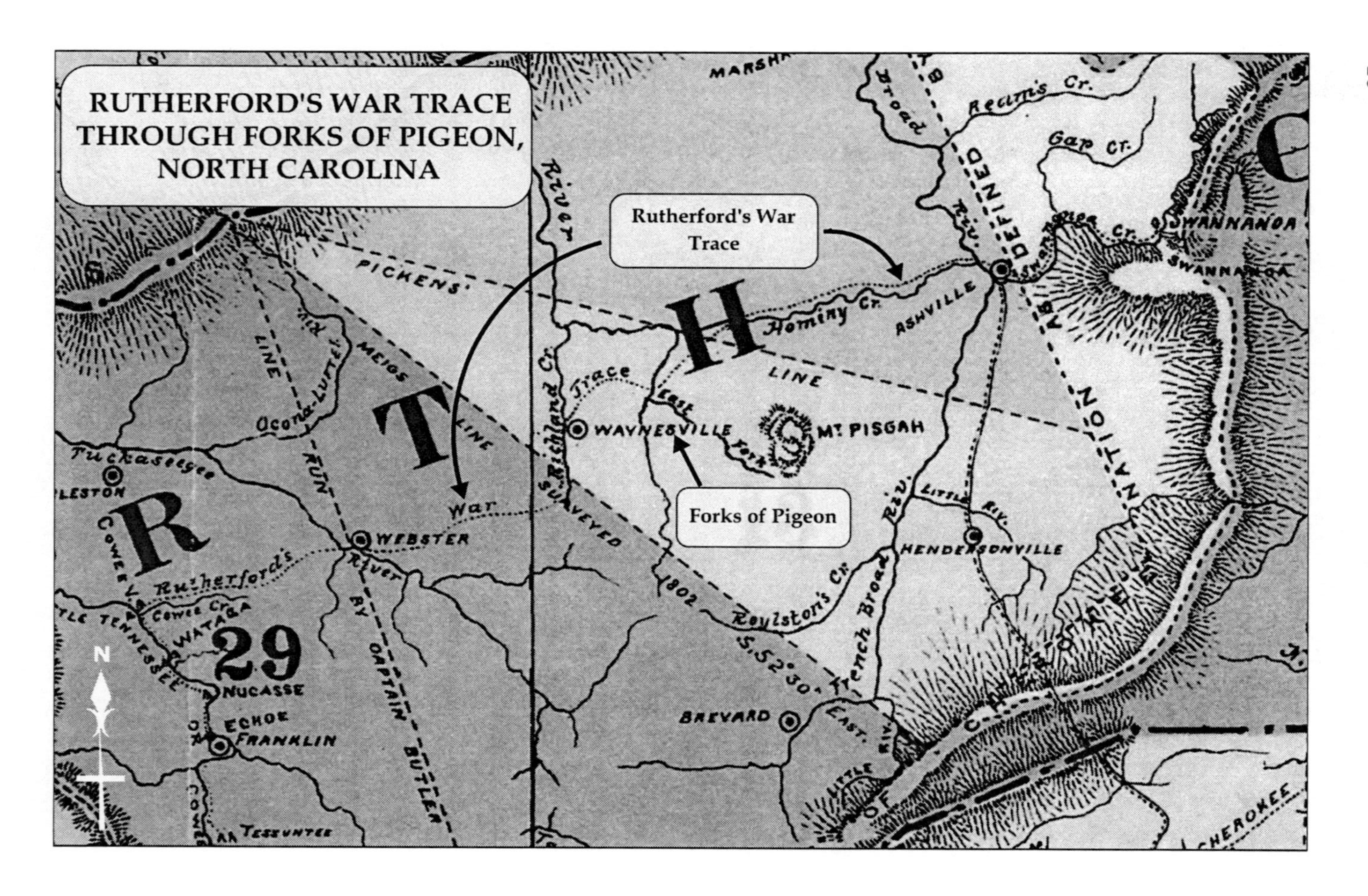
RUTHERFORD'S WAR TRACE
THROUGH FORKS OF PIGEON,
NORTH CAROLINA
Rutherford's War
Trace
Forks of Pigeon
WAYNESVILLE
MT PISGAH
ASHVILLE
HENDERSONVILLE
BREVARD
WEBSTER
FRANKLIN
NUCASSE
ECHOE
WATAGA
TESSUNTEE
DEFINED
NATION
PICKENS'
MEIGS
LINE
SURVEYED
1802
S. 52°30' EAST.
BY CAPTAIN BUTLER
RUN
Hominy Cr.
Richland Cr.
River
Broad
Gap Cr.
Reems Cr.
SWANNANOA
French Broad
Little Riv.
Reulston's Cr.
East
Fork
Trace
War
Rutherford's
Tuckaseegee
Ocona-Luftee Riv.
TENNESSEE
COWEE
Cowee Cr.
CHEROKEE
MARSH
H
T
R
29
N

1 Rutherford's Expedition

Once, many years ago, a great army penetrated the rugged and remote mountains of western North Carolina on a military punitive action against the Cherokee People. The path of this 1776 expedition snaked from the eastern frontier slopes of the Blue Ridge Range over high ridges and through deep river valleys to the farthest western mountains of the state. Led by General Griffith Rutherford, a bellicose contingent of some 2,400 soldiers and Catawba Indians blazed a course smack through Haywood County's Pigeon Valley wilderness.

Today a few highway historic markers indicate the location of the army's old "war trace" at strategic gaps in the mountains, such as Pigeon and Balsam Gaps. The route also paralleled prominent watercourses, including Hominy Creek and the Pigeon River, as signs testify. Mountain dwellers and hordes of tourists traveling through have certainly seen these trace markers. And many have actually pulled off to the side of the road and stopped to read the finer narrative and learn that General Rutherford's "trace" was somewhere in the vicinity. But curious onlookers will certainly be left to wonder why our state's militiamen were fighting Indians and not the British during the early days of the American Revolution. Few modern-day readers will comprehend the reasons or consequences of General Rutherford's bold action and the important role it played in the outcome of the Revolutionary War, the settlement of the mountain frontier, and the eventual removal of the Cherokee Indians to the West.

The significance of the year 1776, of course, is not lost on most Americans. It marked the beginning of the Revolutionary War—the year that the original thirteen colonies declared their independence after years of oppression and dominance by an English colonial government. The Cherokee Indians, who in 1754 had sided with the French against Britain during the French and Indian War, chose to ally with the British at the outset of the American War of Independence. Their frustration at continuing encroachments by white settlers into their mountain lands, even though King George's Proclamation of 1763 prohibited white trespass west of the Blue Ridge, drove them into England's welcoming arms.

Empowered by the Crown and royal treaties, the Cherokees began demanding the withdrawal of the white settlers from all their lands west of the Blue Ridge Mountain range. When these demands went unheeded the Indians initiated a series of raiding actions in May 1776 against the white settlements along the mountain frontier fringes, resulting in the killing of thirty-seven pioneer men and women. Soon news of these atrocities reached General Griffith Rutherford in North Carolina's Rowan County. One of six brigadier generals commissioned by the state's new Provincial Congress, Rutherford was in charge of the militia in the Salisbury District and immediately began raising an army to take retaliatory measures against the Indians.

After assembling an army of two thousand fighting white men, several hundred sympathetic Catawba Indians, and the necessary supply resources for a forty-day operation, General Rutherford struck out on September 1, 1776, from Davidson's Fort (near the present-day town of Old Fort) and marched into the forbidding wilderness habitation of the Cherokees. Not unexpectedly, the Indians fled before the imposing American forces and were not easily brought to battle. The armed troops systematically destroyed numerous vacated Indian villages, granaries, and crops in the fields along the Tuckasegee, Hiwassee, Valley, Oconaluftee, and Little Tennessee River valleys. Anything and everything of import to the Cherokees was burned or ruined to further their depredation and destroy their ability to wage war.

General Rutherford and his men met with little opposition, and as a result casualties were light on both sides. There were several skirmishes, however, with perhaps the fiercest of these occurring at Wayah Bald Gap near today's town of Franklin. After about a month of this scorched-earth warfare, and believing their mission accomplished and the Cherokee Nation severely punished, General Rutherford's weary band retraced their pathway out of the mountains and back to the safety of Davidson's Fort. Orders were given for the route to be marked and blazed, and subsequently the "Rutherford Trace" was to be forever known and would become a crucial gateway for white settlers moving into the remote mountain fastnesses.[1]

The Indians had indeed suffered an enormous loss and were greatly weakened and demoralized by Rutherford's stunning action. They would become disillusioned, as well, with broken English promises to restore their lost lands, and would soon treat with the American republic, ceding more rights and giving away additional Indian land to the fledgling nation. There would now be no stopping of the American pioneer migration into western North Carolina's frontier wilderness. The white appetite for the verdant, well-watered lands and virgin forests of the Cherokee territory had been whetted, and the Indians and English were powerless before the relentless onslaught of Scots-Irish, German, and English settlers hungry for new land to homestead.

The Pigeon Valley was among those beautiful, pristine river valleys that the army encountered on its destructive incursion into Cherokee territory. They reached it by initially penetrating the Blue Ridge through a crack in the range known today as the Swannanoa Gap (railroad engineers would choose the same gap to breach those rugged mountain walls a century later). Through this opening the legion trudged and directly came upon the Swannanoa River, its meandering course leading them through the area south of today's Asheville (where in the late nineteenth century George Vanderbilt would create his magnificent Biltmore Estate), and eventually guiding them to its confluence with the French Broad River.

General Rutherford's army forded the French Broad, one of the world's oldest rivers and one of only two in the United States that flow north, at a point thereafter known as the "War Ford." Close by, on the west bank of the grand river, they came across a tributary stream which was promptly named Hominy Creek. The expeditionary train of soldiers, Indians, and pack horses followed this lazy watercourse through unspoiled woodlands, meadows, and hillsides that have since been transformed into today's communities of Sand Hill, Enka, and Candler. As the Hominy's breadth narrowed and flow quickened, the army relentlessly pursued it to its source in Haywood County.

Near Hominy Creek's headwaters General Rutherford and his troops abandoned its course and crossed a low ridge to enter the drainage area of the Pigeon River and surrounding Pigeon Valley. In the vicinity where the Ford of Pigeon settlement was later made and eventually Canton was to be founded, the army first encountered the Pigeon River. So historic was this event, and long remembered, that one early land deed in the Haywood County records uses "a point at the Ford of Pigeon where a great army once crossed" as the legal bound of the property description. Canton citizens may be surprised that a "great army" once marched through their fair town and along its riverbanks during the Revolutionary War.[2]

But Rutherford's expedition did not actually cross the Pigeon River in the Canton vicinity, as the old land record indicates. The army proceeded up the Pigeon Valley along the east bank of the river through lush, fertile bottomland where the farming community of Bethel thrives today. Then, discovering a westerly route out of the Pigeon drainage basin, the expedition crossed over the river just below the point where the East and West forks of the river are joined—later to be known as Forks of Pigeon—and escaped the Valley through the Pigeon Gap. Several decades later the early county fathers and road builders would utilize this strategic cleft as they laid out one of the first public roads that connected Waynesville and Forks of Pigeon; it is the same place where modern-day U.S. Highway 276 crosses the divide. Leaving the Pigeon Valley behind, General Rutherford continued his hunt for the Cherokees along Richland Creek and across Balsam Gap into the wild river valleys and highlands beyond.

General Rutherford's punitive expedition did not destroy the Cherokee Nation, but it did serve to undermine its fighting capacity and break its spirit. Afterward the eastern Indians would cease to be a major force to reckon with during the Revolution, and their leverage at future treaty tables was significantly diminished. They were forced to relinquish vast areas of their ancient tribal lands through one treaty after another with the American government until their final expulsion to Indian Territory west of the Mississippi River. This Cherokee exodus from western North Carolina's mountains in 1838 and 1839, often referred to as the "Trail of Tears," has gained considerable infamy over the years as an example of the United States government's misguided policies toward Native American peoples as it pursued its Manifest Destiny.

Undoubtedly, some of the general's soldiers were struck with the natural beauty and enormous potential of the western mountains and would return just a few years later at the conclusion of the war to lay claim to vast plots of fertile farming ground along the Pigeon

River. One such pioneer was Jacob Shook (my fourth great-grandfather), who was one of Haywood County's very early white settlers and prominent citizens. Jacob built a prosperous farm close by the banks of the Pigeon near today's town of Clyde, where he is reputed to have constructed the first frame house in the county.[3]

Although today one cannot readily see physical evidence of Rutherford's trace through the Pigeon Valley, early records account for his passage along the Pigeon River as he groped westward in search of the wily Cherokee Indians. Historical markers dot our modern macadam traces that wind through the western North Carolina mountains to remind us of his stern action in a century long past. And only the ancient mountains stand witness to a time when a great army of Patriot Indian fighters and Catawba Indians, armed only with flintlock muskets, hunting knives, and tomahawks, prowled the Pigeon Valley in search of the Cherokee.

Opposite: "Gift from the Heavens," watercolor by Jo Ridge Kelley, 2003. Used by permission.

2 Winter: Pigeon Valley Visions

THE EARLY PIONEER SETTLERS of the Pigeon Valley area began moving into the remote mountain region around 1800. Finding their way through passes in the Blue Ridge wall, in an area where peaks rise to more than 5,000 feet, they arrived mostly on foot or horseback anxious to tame the beautiful wilderness surrounding the Pigeon River and to forge new lives for themselves.

Often I wonder about the challenges and struggles that those first Valley farmers must have endured. There were, of course, forests to be cleared and log shelters to be built; there was ground to be broken and cultivated and food to be procured or produced. And months of harsh, inhospitable winter weather would have presented crucial tests of their capabilities and character and grave threats to human survival. By closing my eyes and mentally turning back the clock a century or more, I try to imagine how those mountaineer families coped and endured the bone-chilling cold and their primitive living circumstances.

When I make this trip back in time I can visualize . . .

• *brisk winds and cold blowing through the Valley, causing eyes and noses to water and earlobes and cheeks to turn rosy*

• *fields lying fallow and bare under low, gray skies, the earth broken only by the intrusions of corn stubbles, winter grasses, and ragged shocks of cornstalks and fodder*

• *the entire Valley glistening and white from a heavy rime coating and stubbornly resisting the thawing urges of an early morning sun*

• *snowdrifts piled high against the barn and the lonely privy, and narrow traces of footprints leading to and from those vital structures*

• *neighboring families coming together at hog-killing time—a happy affair designed to render fattened swine into nutritional meats and useful fats that would see them through the months ahead*

• *a deep blanket of snow and ice concealing a small creek, except in the swiftest runs where it dares to gurgle and make its escape*

• *the chickens holed up in the coop and the cow and old mule content in the barn as the snow continues to fall, while the quietness grows ever quieter and the whiteness ever whiter*

• mighty, majestic hemlocks whose long evergreen boughs strain and bend under the weight of a fresh wet snow

• a rustic little cabin with its puncheon floor that offers nary respite for little cold bare feet

• bears safely sheltered under huge rocks and inside cozy dens, unconscious of the raging winter blizzards and howling winds

• the Valley's families readied for a long, hard winter, with the corn crib overflowing, apples and taters buried in the ground, and leather-britches dried and put away

• in the gray sky far across the Valley and along the ridges, thin ribbons of bluish smoke curling upwards from distant neighbors' chimneys

• a young boy digging up frozen ground and straw to reclaim taters and apples hidden away for keeping

• a pioneer farmer, awakened early before the sun's rays bend over the horizon, wading hurriedly through snow to a tiny privy

• a young girl in dawn's early light breaking the ice over a frozen spring to fetch water for her mother, all the while taking great care to keep hands and feet warm and dry

• women waking before all others to fire up the

cook stove and start the pork meat frying and the coffee boiling

• *women bundled in homespun from head to toe, stooped over the hearth, prodding coals back to life around a Dutch oven filled with cornbread batter*

• *a stick of unseasoned wood hissing and popping and spewing on the hearth fire*

• *happy, bright-eyed children wrapped in homespun and animal skins, huddling around the fireside as they wiggle their toes and push bare feet closer to the warmth*

• *young'uns flopped down on a bear skin on the floor to read by the fire's light and warm by its flame*

• *families gathered around the warm hearth laughing and talking as the corn pops and chestnuts roast under the hot coals*

• *boys and girls sleeping cozily in the loft beneath heavy animal hides while snowflakes, blown by the wind between rived roof boards, fall onto their innocent little heads*

• *a horse-drawn farm sled on sourwood runners gliding roughly over frozen roads and trails, loaded down with the Yule log, a scrawny pine Christmas tree, and merry children whooping and hollering all the way*

- *a meager yet meaningful Christmas celebration with few presents—maybe an orange or two and a mother's homemade craftwork—and grateful children and thankful parents on whom the significance of this special day is not lost.*

I can clearly see all these winter visions and many more when reflecting on life in the Valley early on. Perhaps the reader will have glimpsed them, too, and will have gained an appreciation for the hardy folk who came before us and settled the Pigeon Valley, both enduring and enjoying those long winters long ago.

Captain William Harrison (Hack) Hargrove, hailed as Canton's "first citizen," led a most eventful and fruitful life highlighted by an admirable Civil War record and distinguished service in various political and professional pursuits. (Family photograph, c. 1880s. Collection of the author.)

3 Captain Hack

A Story of the Life of William Harrison Hargrove and His Contributions to the Welfare of Haywood County

"A Useful Citizen Filled with Honor Has Gone to Reward"

THE WORDS ABOVE, from a long forgotten newspaper obituary, caught my attention a few years ago while rummaging through old genealogy records. Upon reading further, I saw that this was an account of my great-grandfather William Harrison (Hack) Hargrove's passing almost a century earlier.[1] Of course I was not unfamiliar with Hack, having heard my mother and her sisters talk about him often. I knew he was a Civil War veteran, but beyond that details of his life and history were rather murky. As I continued to scan Hack's obituary and learn about his life's occupations and achievements, the more fascinated I became. Not only was he a veteran of the South's war for independence, but at one time or another he had been a farmer, teacher, county surveyor, county commissioner, state legislator, agent of the Western North Carolina Railroad, real estate agent, leader of the state's temperance movement, and newspaper editor. The newspaper recorded that he had been "closely identified with the affairs of the county, especially in the welfare and development of Canton." When finished reading the article, I put it aside and paused to contemplate the breadth and productivity of the life that Hack Hargrove had lived.

My father once told me that everyone should strive to leave footprints behind as evidence of their existence and worthy achievements. There were no doubts that my great-grandfather had left many footprints, and I resolved to uncover them and discover where they might lead.

The Formative Years

In the early to mid-1800s the fertile valley surrounding the Pigeon River where its two tributary streams collide hosted a farming settlement known as Forks of Pigeon; it was into this community that William Harrison Hartgrove was born on January 31, 1841. His father, Augustus Columbus Hartgrove, was the son of William Manson Hartgrove, the first Hartgrove to enter Haywood County, in about 1823. Ellen Childress, his mother, hailed from neighboring Buncombe County. She was the daughter of Samuel Childress, who had relocated to that county from Tennessee.

William was the firstborn child of Augustus and Ellen, and within only a brief span of years he would gain several siblings: Joseph

Franklin, born 1844; Mary (Mollie), born 1848; Augustus Alexander, born 1850; and Althea Caroline, born 1853. Another brother, Thomas, died at the age of one year; a sister, Amanda, died as an infant.[2]

William's formative years growing up in Forks of Pigeon would certainly have been spent laboring away at farm chores on his father's little homestead, in addition to helping tend the younger brothers and sisters. For a period of time Augustus and his family probably lived in a small log cabin located in what is now known as Peter's Cove.[3] Later Augustus moved the family to a piece of land along the East Fork of the Pigeon River where he worked as a plantation overseer for an absentee landowner, Thomas Lenoir, and his son, Thomas Isaac Lenoir.[4]

Most farms in the Forks of Pigeon region during that era were small concerns that grew principally corn and wheat crops. William would have spent most of the daylight hours during the growing season at work in the fields—clearing, plowing, planting, and harvesting, and then repeating the yearly cycle again. In addition he would have lent his growing mind and developing muscles to help his mother with the domestic burdens and endeavors. Her lot was not inconsiderable: it included caring for the babies, cooking, tending the gardens, and producing household necessities such as preserves, butter, quilts, and clothing. There was plentiful work and activity to keep the Valley's young boys occupied during the spring, summer, and fall, and William would not have escaped these responsibilities.

The little schooling the children received during William's youthful years occurred during the late fall and winter months. A relatively new two-room schoolhouse had been built by then and stood near where the Bethel Middle School is located today. William's grandfather, William Manson Hartgrove, produced the brick and constructed the massive fireplaces and chimneys that anchored each end of the structure.[5] It is likely that William attended several sessions at this school. Records reveal that his father then sent him over to Waynesville to attend the private school of John M. McIver for more advanced study.[6] William's future achievements and the professions that he pursued indicate that he acquired a level of education uncommon to the rural community in which he lived.

All of William's scholarly learning and innate reasoning capacity would be tapped as his twentieth birthday loomed and passed. Events and decisions involving states' rights, slavery, and secession were transpiring across the nation and would soon affect those mountaineers residing within the remote Forks of Pigeon community. In late 1860 and the first half of 1861 one rebellious Southern state after another voted to secede from the United States of America, joining together in an independent confederacy to form the Confederate States of America. Throughout the South young men were being asked to take up arms to defend their states and the Southern "cause." And when this debate reached Haywood County's mountain fastness a youthful William Hartgrove was forced to contemplate these serious matters, weigh his loyalties, and make a difficult and far-reaching decision.

A Mountain-bred Rebel

After wavering for several months North Carolina finally voted in May 1861 to secede from the Union. The sentiment in Haywood County was not completely pro-secession, and many citizens remained loyal to the Union throughout the war. But the county moved quickly in forming volunteer companies to defend their homeland from Yankee invaders, and William joined with a group of Haywood County men in a company that Joseph Cathey and Captain Thomas Isaac Lenoir were assembling. On July 18, 1861, William, his neighbors, and county brethren, all filled with patriotic fervor and convinced that the war would be one of short duration in which the South would most assuredly gain independence from the Northern states, marched off to Asheville, North Carolina. At that town, the largest in the western North Carolina highlands, their company was designated as Company F and was combined with nine other mountain companies to form what later became the 25th Regiment North Carolina Infantry Troops, in the service of the Confederate States of America.[7]

The men began to learn the rudiments of being a soldier at Asheville's Camp Patton and Camp Clingman, training there for several weeks. In mid-September 1861 William's regiment struck camp and marched eastward across the Blue Ridge to Morganton, North Carolina, the western terminus of the railroad system in the state during the Civil War. At Morganton, where many of those mountaineer soldiers eyed a train for the first time, the troops embarked on the cars for eastern North Carolina and for an interminable war more horrific than any could have foreseen.

William served for the duration of the Civil War with the 25th North Carolina Regiment after boarding that train in 1861. During the first year William's unit saw very little combat action as it was assigned coastal defensive duty at Grahamville, South Carolina, and later in eastern North Carolina, where Private Hartgrove was promoted to sergeant. From June 1862 until the end of the year his regiment was attached to Robert E. Lee's Army of Northern Virginia and participated in some of the most ferocious fighting of the war at the Seven Days' Battles around Richmond, Virginia; the Battle of Antietam at Sharpsburg, Maryland; and the Battle of Fredericksburg, Virginia. Apparently escaping these conflicts without serious injury, Sergeant Hartgrove and his regiment of mountain boys returned to eastern North Carolina in January 1863. For the ensuing fifteen months the 25th North Carolina remained primarily in the coastal regions of North Carolina and Virginia, protecting strategic railroads and Southern commercial interests.

In early 1864 the Northern stranglehold on the South was gradually tightening. General Ulysses S. Grant's Union armies were beginning another push toward the Confederate capital city of Richmond, Virginia. The 25th North Carolina was ordered in May 1864 to rush to the Richmond defense lines to help stave off Federal assaults against Richmond and Petersburg. Thereafter, through March 1865, William Hartgrove manned the defensive works and trenches with his regiment in front of those besieged cities. Holed up for more than nine months in the hideous red saps, the mountain-bred troops of the 25th North Carolina Regiment fought off countless Federal attacks, endured enemy sharpshooter fire and artillery shelling on a daily basis, and suffered unfathomable personal deprivations.

During most of this period of trench warfare the Confederate soldiers were ill-fed and unpaid, and some were without shoes and warm clothes to resist the cold winter weather of 1864–65. Moreover, the mountain boys were regularly receiving letters from home with news that their families were also starving and that gangs of deserters, Tories, and draft evaders were roaming the hills and bushwhacking innocent folk living in isolated regions. Contained within many of these letters was rhetoric filled with pathetic pleas for the men to return to their families and loved ones. The pressures that came to bear on those remaining few mountain rebels in the Petersburg ditches were unbearable to many: approximately one in five of the 25th North Carolina Regiment's soldiers deserted.

Sergeant William Hartgrove was never among that number. Promoted to first lieutenant in August 1864, he saw the thing through and participated with his regiment in the fighting at the battles of Drewry's Bluff, the Crater, Weldon Railroad, Fort Stedman, and finally Five Forks. The Battle of Five Forks on April 1, 1865, occurred on the southwestern side of Petersburg, where Union infantry and cavalry forces massed and finally broke through General Robert E. Lee's defensive lines. Some five thousand Confederate prisoners were taken in that action. One of those so unfortunate was First Lieutenant William Hartgrove.

In his book *The Annals of Haywood County, North Carolina,*

First Lieutenant William Harrison Hartgrove served with the Confederate Army's 25th Regiment North Carolina Infantry Troops through the entire Civil War. (Family photograph, c. 1864. Collection of the author.)

W. C. Allen gives the following account: "During the battle of Five Forks he [Hargrove] rescued Lieutenant G. S. Ferguson, who was desperately wounded. In the affair, however, he was himself captured and sent as a prisoner to Sandusky, Ohio. He was released in June, 1865, and returned to Haywood County."

Although Allen makes references elsewhere to "Captain Hargrove," there is no evidence in extant Confederate records that William Hartgrove was ever promoted to the rank of captain. However, in the latter months of 1864 he signed the company muster rolls as commander of the company, likely indicating that Capt.

James Blaylock was absent at the time. First Lieutenant Hartgrove was sent to the Johnson Island prisoner-of-war camp near Sandusky, Ohio, where he remained until the conclusion of the war. After the final surrender of the several Confederate armies in the field had occurred and after he signed an oath of allegiance to the United States of America on June 18, 1865, the young lieutenant was released and allowed to go home.[8]

It took William a full three weeks to make the trek home from Ohio to Forks of Pigeon. His personal diary provides the record of his odyssey.[9]

— Left Sandusky, Ohio on June 19th on train
Traveled by train through Newark, Ohio to Bellairs, Virginia to Martinsburg, Virginia and then to Baltimore, Maryland on 20th

— Left Baltimore on 21st on a stock boat
Traveled on stock boat down Chesapeake Bay to Fort Monroe, Virginia arriving on 22nd

— Left Fort Monroe on 23rd on stock boat
Traveled on stock boat up the James River to City Point, Virginia and then to Pittsburg Landing, Virginia arriving on 23rd

— Stopped off in Petersburg, Virginia to look in on friends in hospital. Found all OK except G. S. Ferguson who was improving. [William stayed over in Petersburg waiting on his friend Garland Ferguson to get well enough so that he could take him home. After waiting until July 5 and then learning that it would be another three weeks before Ferguson could travel, William decided to continue his trip home alone.]

— Left Petersburg on July 5th on train
Traveled by train to Danville, Virginia arriving on July 5th

— Left Danville on July 6th on train
Traveled by train to Greensboro, North Carolina and then to Salisbury, North Carolina arriving on July 6th

- Left Salisbury on July 7th by train
  Traveled by train to Morganton, North Carolina arriving on July 7th
- Left Morganton on July 7th at 9pm and arrived home on July 10th at 3pm [William most likely made this last leg of the journey on foot and possibly in wagons that he managed to catch rides on.]

It is a testament to William's character that he stopped off in Petersburg to check on friends recovering from wounds and sickness in the hospitals there. He steadfastly remained at the side of the injured Garland Ferguson for almost two weeks, waiting to assist his good friend home. It seems that there were no sacrifices too great for those brave young Southern soldiers who had endured such a terrible war. They fought side by side, slept and ate together, and looked after one another. The bonds that developed were stronger than those of blood brothers.

From his later reminiscences it can reasonably be concluded that William returned from the battlefields bearing mental burdens from his wartime experiences and harboring bitter sentiments toward the men from the South, and the North for that matter, who had led the country into a civil war. These intimate feelings he sheltered closely, yet evidence revealing them was left recorded in his personal notes and diary. The following short excerpt gives a hint of the troubled thoughts he held:

> Arrived home from this bloody ruthless and unjust war with a very sad heart with the thought of leaving so many dear friends behind me, never again to return.[10]

William Hartgrove leaves no doubt as to his thoughts on the war experience. The "illegitimate influences" to which he refers are the newspapers and "big-mouth politicians" he criticizes elsewhere.

> In this war just ended I have known many who did not want to enlist or volunteer, but were influenced by some of the above illegitimate influences and now their bones are bleaching far from home or friends and their graves erased, not even a board to mark the lonely spot and now many of those same persons who influenced them into war are now condemning those poor unfortunate creatures and branding them as hot headed rebels. This is the pay you get for not saying "No". [11]

Many thousands of other Southern rebel soldiers would be similarly traumatized and carry home with them significant mental and physical scars from the Civil War battlefields. William wrote that he arrived at home "and found all right at home and thank the good Lord for my safe return to my good home."[12] Four long years of his life had been consumed by the terrible war, but the still youthful mountaineer would surely have been anxious for a return to normalcy and the prospects of resuming civilian life and starting afresh.

A Fresh Beginning

The Pigeon Valley to which William returned following the Civil War was much changed from the region he had left four years earlier. Fields lay fallow and overgrown with briars and thistle. Roads had not been maintained and were scarcely passable. Homes and barns were derelict, in a state of neglect and ruin uncommon to the proud citizens that made the scenic river valley their home. All of these conditions were the consequence of the extended absence of the many young men who had left their families and homes behind to defend their homeland. But those native sons were now back at home—the fortunate ones who had survived—and they quickly began the work of making the fields productive again and rebuilding their community and their lives.[13]

William presumably resided in the Augustus Hartgrove homestead immediately after his return from the war and helped his father and brothers raise corn and wheat crops. In his notebook he indicates that he also tried his hand at teaching school in the Forks of Pigeon community.[14] In 1867 he opened and taught a subscription school session at Chincapin Grove schoolhouse, and in August 1869 another three-month subscription school at Chincapin is noted. Additional records show that William began teaching three classes (designated "Class 1st," "Class 2nd," and "Minor Class") at the Bethel schoolhouse on November 22, 1869. A total of approximately thirty scholars, including his sister Althea, attended that school session. William's notebook, which covers a brief period following the war, is packed full of tidbits, scribblings, and records that he jotted down in pencil and ink. There is evidence of a "Kentucky Campaign," as the young journalist styled it, lasting from October 9 until about December 1, 1866. He accompanied Thomas Isaac Lenoir on this journey to Lexington, Kentucky, where his former captain sold and purchased livestock. William records that he "Left home on 9th Oct. 1866, Traveled by way of Asheville, Pt. [Paint] Rock & the Green[e]ville road to within 8 miles of Green[e]ville Tenn & turned to the left & crossed Chucky at Allen's Bridge." From this point he lists the several communities and river crossings that he encountered along the way to Lexington, Kentucky, as well as the distances he traveled.

It also appears from the faint pages of the notebook that William

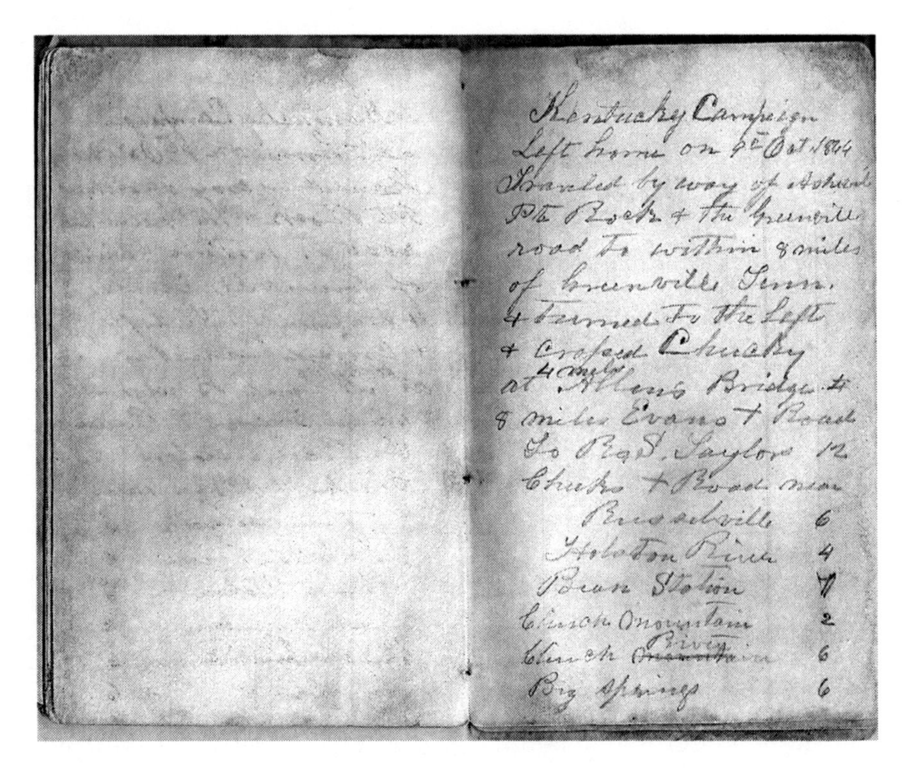

Kentucky Campaign
Left home on 8th Oct 1866
Traveled by way of Asheville
Pt. Rock & the Greenville
road to within 8 miles
of Greenville Tenn.
& turned to the left
& crossed Chucky
at Allens Bridge 4 miles
8 miles Evans & Road
To Rod. Taylors 12
Chucky & Road near
Russelville 6
Holston River 4
Bean Station 7
Clinch Mountain 2
Clinch River 6
Big Springs 6

Hack Hartgrove's personal notebook has survived the years to offer a glimpse into his life during the period immediately following the Civil War. On this page Hack recorded the start of his "Kentucky Campaign" to Louisville in 1866. (Collection of the author.)

and some friends in 1867 founded a social club, despite the difficult postwar circumstances. On one page, under the heading "Ben Franklin's" and the date of February 6, 1867, are listed the names of club members along with credits and debits for initiation fees. The group may have been fashioned after the famous Junto which Ben Franklin himself once formed with young friends to discuss topics of the day. Franklin's club was dedicated to mutual improvement, which may also have been the inspiration of William and his cohorts Jo F. Cathey, A. J. Long, D. B. Nelson, and R. A. Sentelle.

Some years later the Rev. D. B. Nelson became the first grand master of the Masonic Lodge in Waynesville and a principal at Bethel Academy. R. A. Sentelle would become the first county superintendent of schools. It is possible that William's club was a forum for these up-and-coming young leaders to discuss politics, reconstruction issues, and other topics of shared interest.

Other notations in the journal record expenses incurred on trips to the markets in Greenville, South Carolina and Augusta, Georgia. His scribbled lines include expenses for tolls, corn and fodder, horse collars, a wagon axle tree, sugar, and cheese. These market treks normally took about one month's time to complete, and William made several of them over the years until the railroad finally penetrated the mountains.

Throughout the remaining pages of the log book are numerous notations inserted in a random manner which give some insight into the times and the young man's life. A sampling of these is presented below:

> Boar had a calf July 20th 1870
> Disease took the Jack
> Rose took the bull Augt 17th 1870
>
> Christmas Day Dec 25th 1866
> Frost bitten snow last night & cool today
>
> Christmas Day 1867
> Nice & pleasant spent part of the day at Mr. Chambers and the night at Col. J. Cathey's
>
> Deliver the mules to John Summey if he will receive them & the money

> $475.00. Two one hundred dollar bills U.S. legal tender & at least $175.00 in small bills.
>
> On April 14th, 1870 Jimmie Brown set in to work for a period of one month beginning at 12:00 at a salary of $4.50 per month.
>
> Mr Brown sent two head of cattle here January 5th to winter at 50 cts/per head per month. Took them away March 25th.

The treasure trove of information gleaned from William's little book opens a window into his life during the first several years following the war. A glance through it has revealed much about the young man's efforts to rid himself of Civil War demons and to overcome the difficulties that he must have encountered with Reconstruction policies and hardships. Unrevealed in his annotations, however, is the fortunate discovery of a partner to share life's burdens and future challenges—one who would play a vital role in the establishment of yet another Hargrove-Cathey family in the valley of the Forks of Pigeon settlement.

Another Hargrove and Cathey Union

William married Nancy Louisa Cathey on November 9, 1869. Nannie, as most knew her, was the daughter of William Burton Cathey and Lucinda Moore, and the granddaughter of Col. Joseph Cathey. The Cathey family was one of the very early settler families to arrive in Haywood County, around 1800. William Cathey, Nancy's great-grandfather, broke through the mountain ramparts with the first wave of pioneers and was among the first to settle on the banks of the Pigeon River, near the fork of the east and west branches of

William and Nannie Hartgrove took up residence in this house for a year or two after their marriage in 1869. It was originally a log construction built by Nannie's parents, William Burton and Lucinda Moore Cathey, about 1849. Later it was expanded and clad with sawn boards, as shown here. The house survived for almost 150 years before being demolished in the latter years of the twentieth century. (Photo circa 1980; collection of the author.)

that river. William Hartgrove's grandfather had found his way into the North Carolina mountains in about 1823 and established the Hartgrove family roots in the Pigeon Valley. It was from this pioneer stock that the young William Hartgrove and Nancy Cathey were descended. Their marriage was just one of many Hargrove-Cathey unions that occurred over the years in the Pigeon Valley, producing solid working citizens who contributed to the development and prosperity of the community.[15]

Immediately after making their nuptial promises, the young couple moved in with Nancy's widowed mother, Lucinda Moore Cathey. The house in which they lived was situated on the west side of the Pigeon River (in today's Cathey Cove), near a large tract of Moore land on which Lucinda Moore was raised. During that first growing season, William, along with a hired hand by the name of Jimmie Brown, raised his first crops on a piece of Moore property. One might assume, due to the month-long trip to Augusta that William made and recorded in the fall of 1870, that he produced surplus crops that could be traded and sold in the foreign markets.[16] Not to be outdone that first harvest season, Nancy produced the fruit of their marriage union with the birth of their first child, James Burton, on October 26, 1870.

The record shows that William built "some" cabins on the Moore place and moved into them during the winter of 1871 and 1872. The use of the plural terms may refer to a livestock shed or barn, in addition to a small log cabin. Apparently the cabin was not completed, nor was the shed yet ready to shelter animals, because he wrote: ". . . moved to them [the cabins] on 29th of Feb. 1872 and then fell a snow 15 in. deep which found us in poor condition to receive it as we had no stables nor cracks filled in our cabin."[17] It is difficult to contemplate the hardships the couple and their child must have suffered.

Poor Nancy, being a dutiful wife and companion, faithfully followed her husband in the midst of a cold winter, baby in tow, to live in a log enclosure which had no mud-filling in the log chinks. During that late February blizzard mentioned in the journal, Nancy and one-year old James were surely exposed to freezing wintry drafts in the dark cabin interior. But the young family survived somehow, and as spring finally crept into the Forks of Pigeon valley there was more than warmer weather to be thankful for. On April 15, 1872, in a small, rustic log cabin perched on a mountainside overlooking the Pigeon River, Florence Leona, the couple's second child, poked her head into the world for the very first time.

During the 1872 growing season William managed to purchase a parcel of land, regarding which he wrote: "Made a crop on the Moore place but in fall found myself a good deal in debt for land & no visible means to get out." Apparently it would not be long before William discovered a way out of his worrisome indebtedness. He found work with Nancy's grandfather, Col. Joseph Cathey, earning the handsome wage of sixteen dollars per month.[18]

After a brief period of employment with Colonel Cathey, running from December 4, 1872, until January 24, 1874, William resumed farming and raised another bumper crop for which he recorded the number of bushels of corn and wheat and the fact that it "was a nice income." At least two significant family events marked the year of 1874. A third child, Joseph Alexander, was born to William and Nancy on April 12. On a much more sorrowful note, the Forks of Pigeon community was plunged into grief and mourning when one of its most revered residents was lost to them. Colonel Joseph Cathey died on June 1, 1874, after a fruitful and unparalleled life of exceptional accomplishment.

County records reveal that in September 1874 Lucinda deeded another forty-three-acre tract of land from her Moore holdings to her daughter, Nancy. Quite possibly it was the same piece of land where the young Hartgroves' crude log cabins were located. In the winter of 1875–76 William made two trips to the Augusta market in the company of his double brother-in-law, James Webster Cathey (sister Althea's husband and Nannie's brother).[19] When they returned from the second of these trips in late January 1876, William found his father gravely ill, and only a short time later, on February 18, Augustus passed away. The widowed Ellen Hargrove would survive her husband for another twenty years.

William recorded that in June of 1876 heavy rains and a Pigeon River "freshet" flooded the whole valley and did tremendous damage to the crops and fields. Undeterred, he replanted the crops which he made in three months, and barely completed the harvest ahead of the first white frost tiptoeing down from the mountains. That winter was one of the worst in memory for those living along the Pigeon Valley, with a low temperature of twenty degrees below zero, the coldest ever recorded for the Forks of Pigeon valley.[20]

The births of Theodore Augustus on June 6, 1877, and William Walter on September 18, 1879, completed William and Nannie Hartgrove's family. By that time they had outgrown the small log cabin and would surely have moved to more spacious quarters on their own land that could accommodate the large family. Farming and making crops remained the primary sources of the family's livelihood, but William's intellectual gifts and personable traits were to open for him entirely different professional pursuits.

A Useful Citizen

As William Hargrove progressed in years most friends, acquaintances, and Valley folk referred to him as "Captain Hack," a fond

Captain William Harrison Hargrove, a "useful citizen," c. 1900. (Collection of the author.)

though informal acknowledgment of his officer rank and distinguished service to the Confederate States of America. There is no evidence to cast light on the origins of the nickname "Hack," which he seems to have adopted among his friends and family. At some point after the war Hartgrove also modified the spelling of his surname, dropping the "t" on occasion. The "Hargrove" spelling is most common and widespread today in Haywood County and beyond. Place names gradually shifted in usage, too, and folks began to substitute "Pigeon Valley" for Forks of Pigeon.

Farming and weather were not the only matters preoccupying Hack Hargrove in 1876. Haywood County records for that year reveal that he was serving on the board of county commissioners. Recorded in the archives is the fact that Hack voted against a commissioners' order to grant to an individual a license to retail spirituous liquors.[21] This is the first instance found of his involvement in county political affairs, the vote demonstrating the strong passion Hack held for the temperance movement. Years later he would rise to the highest level in the state within the Sons of Temperance organization.[22]

In December 1878 Hack was appointed by the county commissioners to a five-person committee "whose duty it should be to devise a plan on which to build a Court House."[23] Obviously Hack had by this time established an excellent reputation for himself, and the other county officials apparently relied on him to insure that a good and reasonable plan for the erection of a new courthouse was produced. Hack's committee fulfilled its obligation, it would seem, as the construction of the third Haywood County courthouse was completed in 1884. The imposing three-story, red-brick building even boasted a clock tower. (It no longer stands, and the present-day courthouse is located on the same site.[24]) For a simple farmer who had a few short years before called a tiny log cabin home, it was an impressive, perhaps surprising, achievement.

The following year, 1879, Hack went before the board of commissioners to "renew his bond as County Surveyor." The bond, in the amount of $500, insured that Hack would reliably and professionally fulfill the responsibilities of the surveyor position, which ran for a term of two years. Having held the position for two years prior, he would continue in the post until his unexplained resignation in 1882.

How Hack might have gotten his start in the surveying profession is not known. He could readily have learned about the county surveyor position, along with the responsibilities of the job, through his work on the county commission as early as 1876 and possibly before that. As a commissioner he would have developed close relationships with influential political and civic leaders of the community that could have helped him gain this post. And it is not unreasonable to believe that his association and strong friendship with Judge Garland Ferguson—whose life he is credited with saving during the Civil War—could have mattered more than anything else. Ferguson became county clerk of superior court soon after the war and went on to become a very successful and prominent lawyer, judge, and state senator. So it would seem that Hack had the political ties and influence to land the key job. But what about the competency and technical skills to perform the work?

The most common role of the land surveyor in Hack's day was to determine the boundaries and area of a given piece of land or the course of a particular road. The surveyor would measure and describe the property boundaries using metes and bounds (distance and direction) measurements. Chains and pins were used to measure distances and a surveyor's compass or theodolite to measure the direction. The most difficult part of the work was recording the property metes and bounds calls geometrically and artistically on a map as well as in a narrative description that could be used in legal property documents. The work required a sufficient knowledge of mathematics and geometry to calculate the area, or acreage, within boundary descriptions. Given the level of education that Hack obtained as a youth and the surveying career that he later forged, it is manifest that he possessed all the required technical skills to perform the highly responsible duties of a county surveyor.

Fording the river was no simple undertaking in Hack Hargrove's hometown of Pigeon River (later Canton). The railroad bridge downriver in the distance helps date the photo to the period between the railroad's arrival in 1882 and the construction of another iron bridge to span the river (in the vicinity of this fording spot) about 1895. (Courtesy Canton Area Historical Museum.)

Captain Hack continued in the county surveyor position until 1882, the year the Western North Carolina Railroad finally breached the imposing ramparts of the Newfound Mountain Range along the eastern boundary of Haywood County, opening the secluded mountainous county to the outside world. No longer did the farmers depend on long droves down the turnpikes to South Carolina and Georgia to reach markets hungry for their grain products, fruit, cattle, and swine. The railroad allowed easy access to the markets beyond the mountains in the North Carolina piedmont and farther on into South Carolina and Virginia. Additionally, local industries such as logging and tanning found the railroad a perfect outlet for their products. Rail service in turn invited other merchants to enter the western mountains and greatly facilitated the travel of tourists desiring to experience the area's beauty and climate.[25]

Haywood County would immediately benefit from the economic boon provided by the new rail transportation system, as would the little hamlet of Pigeon River, located approximately four miles northeast of the Pigeon Valley community. This village, which later adopted the name of Canton, was the western terminus of the railroad for a year or so until construction extended the line on to Clyde and Waynesville. One can easily imagine the level of excitement and activity that surrounded the new railroad station in Pigeon River as it quickly became the commercial focal point of the entire county. Construction of warehouses and other infrastructure to support the passenger and freight service was hurriedly completed for the coming of the first trains. It was paramount that the railroad company find a competent person to manage its affairs at Pigeon River—one possessing a good business head and proven credibility and one with influence in the community. They discovered that a local native by the name of "Captain Hack" Hargrove possessed all these essential qualities, and he was accordingly tapped for the job.

Hack resigned his coveted county surveyor position to become the first Agent for the Western North Carolina Railroad in Pigeon River, N.C., in 1882.[26] He was given total responsibility for running the company's local business and accounting for every passenger and all freight coming in and leaving the station. A statement of account addressed to him in October 1882 from the railroad auditor's office in Salisbury lists the monthly credits and debits for passenger, freight and telegraph services. Freight charges to be collected that month totaled $1,514 and passenger ticket sales totaled $332.

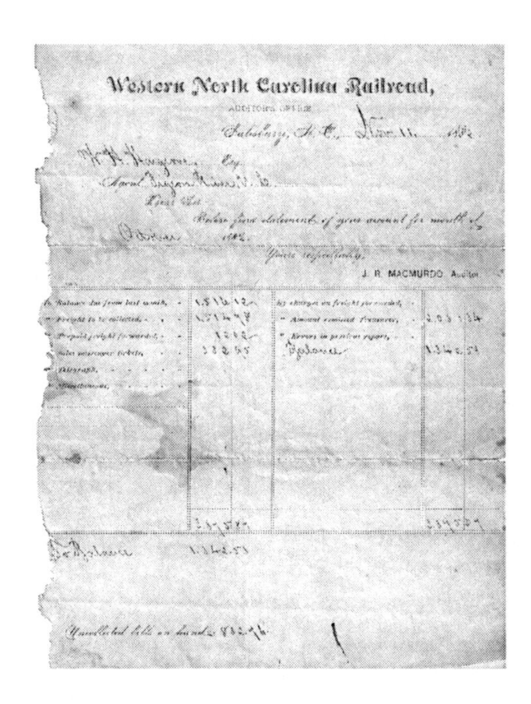
Western North Carolina Railroad,
AUDITOR'S OFFICE
J. R. MACMURDO, Auditor

The Western North Carolina Railroad addressed its monthly statement of account for October 1882 to "W. H. Hargrove, Esq., Agent Pigeon River, N.C." (Collection of the author.)

Hack apparently worked as the railroad agent in Pigeon River for approximately five years. The circumstances or reasons for his leaving the railroad are not clear. However, the railroad company was undergoing a time of fiscal and legal turmoil in 1882. Shortly after its completion to Pigeon River, another railroad, the Richmond & Danville, acquired ownership. For several years thereafter the railroad's ownership rights remained in dispute in the North Carolina State Legislature.[27] This issue would certainly have been distracting, and it could have influenced or forced Hack's retirement from the railroad business some time around 1887.

Shortly after Hack assumed the railroad agent's post his wife, Nannie, died on February 13, 1883. The reasons for her premature death are not known, but the passing of the woman of just thirty-four years surely left Hack, his family and friends, and entire community in a sad state of mourning and grief for an extended period. Not only had Hack lost a woman that he surely loved dearly and a partner with whom he had staked his life's fortunes, but he was now faced with a troublesome dilemma—that of caring for five young children and carrying on with his professional pursuits and political commitments. Hack's mother, Ellen, or mother-in-law, Lucinda, likely moved to the Hargrove home to care for the children. James, Florence, and Joe would have been expected to take on increased responsibilities around the farm and for minding young Theodore and Walter.

In 1885 Hack was again elected to the board of county commissioners and in June of that same year the commissioners appointed him and two other members to constitute a board of education, possibly the first to be formed in Haywood County.[28] The records reveal that in June 1887 "Hack Hargrove came into Commissioner's Court and took the oath of County Surveyor." It is believed that Hack left the employ of the railroad at about this time after no more than five years service, but due to the high degree of influence he had developed in local politics and affairs, he quickly regained the county surveyor post.

County archives indicate that in 1888 Hack once again resigned from an appointed position in the county's service: "Honorable W. H. Hargrove tendered his resignation as a member of the County Board of Education which resignation was accepted with the thanks of this Court in behalf of the educational interest of this County for his valuable services."[29] It is very likely that Hack had no choice in the matter and was forced to resign upon his election in 1888 to represent Haywood County in the lower house of the North Carolina State General Assembly.[30] Undoubtedly he would have traveled to Raleigh by rail to tend to the affairs of the State Assembly, which was in session from January 9 through March 11, 1889. It was probably his first exodus from the mountains to Raleigh since the Civil War. In addition to representing the needs and leanings of Haywood County's population in the work of the Assembly that term, Hack Hargrove surely renewed old friendships and acquaintances with fellow veterans from the days of the Rebellion who were also congregated there.

Hack Hargrove was for many years a Mason in Haywood County. Although little publicized, the Freemasons exercised a strong influence on the county's educational, political, financial, and religious development. In 1866 the first Masonic lodge opened in Waynesville with the Rev. D. B. Nelson elected as the first grand master and Joseph Franklin Hartgrove, Hack's brother, becoming one of the founding members. From this first Waynesville lodge sprang other Masonic lodges at Pigeon River, Clyde, and Sonoma (Pigeon Valley). Hack may have first belonged to the Waynesville lodge, but it is certain that he was a member of the Pigeon River Masonic Lodge and later moved to the Sonoma Lodge when it was created in about 1895. His involvement with the Freemasons, a fraternal organization that professed to "seek to make good men better and thereby make the world a better place in which to live," offered another avenue to improve the welfare of the community. Throughout most of Hack's adult life and until he was buried with Masonic honors, he devoted extreme energies through this organization to better the circumstances of those around him.[31]

During the last decade of the nineteenth century and until his death in 1909, Hack Hargrove's endeavors in political affairs and surveying work continued. He served additional terms as a county commissioner. Existing surveys and plats from this era by his hand give evidence to his continued surveying practice.[32] Contemporary newspaper clippings reveal that he was manager and editor of a news publication called *The Canton Vindicator.*[33] By 1908 the Champion Fibre Company of Hamilton, Ohio, had established and constructed one of the world's largest wood pulp mills in the village of Pigeon River. The town's name was changed to Canton (from the Ohio city that supplied the iron fabrication for the new bridge spanning the river) following the region's tremendous growth to support the huge industrial complex. Canton became a thriving community and the upstart *Canton Vindicator*, a weekly publication, was the first newspaper produced exclusively for the citizenry of the town. At the helm of this fledgling rag was Hack Hargrove, publishing and feeding news and stories of human interest to his good neighbors of Canton and the Pigeon Valley.

Also of interest is the fact that Hack helped found another newspaper in 1908 named *The Haywood Enterprise.* He was an associate editor of this weekly publication that was dedicated primarily to the support of the platform and activities of the Republican Party. Captain Hack's Republican bias ran counter to popular sentiment

CANTON VINDICATOR

hed Every Saturday by the
Vindicator Publishing Co.,
Canton, N. C.

cription price, $1.00 per year
nce.
rtising rates on application.
orrespondence must reach us by
sday night to insure prompt in-

red as second class matter Apr
908, at the post office at Canton,
under act of Congress of March
79.

indebtedness to the Canton
cator for subscription or ad-
ng must be made payable to
. Hargrove, manager and

Folks' Meeting at Canton

7:30 o'clock vast throngs
pouring into Canton in all
of vehicles, horse back and
rians, and continued until 10
, besides the 9:18 train from
ille brought hundreds.

:30 W. T. Sharp convened
y School at Locust Field
, which was well filled. In
eration of the great numbers
harp divided the house into
ections, and asked Prof.
of Asheville, W. H. Har-
and Dr. H. A. Smathers,
one lecture the section as-
them. All lecturing at one
as somewhat like the con.
ng of the languages at the
n of the tower of Babel, but
ned much interested in the

r Sunday School the people
packed as best they could in
rch. The opening song in
Christian Harmony by Dr.
ers. Prayer by Rev. L. B.
fhy, of the Methodist church.
s of welcome by Rev. T. L.

sition in life, as they were nearer according to nature to the haven of rest. His address was much enjoyed and appreciated.

Quartette by Dr. Keedom, E. J. and J. B. Smathers.

An address by Hon. W. G. Candler. As he always makes an interesting address. He took in a wide scope of thought and argument to convince all of the propriety of a better and higher life.

Song by the choir, "Will There be Any Stars in my Crown."

Under the head of business, Rev. W. H. Woodall, of Clyde made a suggestion that a roll book be kept to enroll all above 50 years of age, and that a committee of three with the chairman be appointed for the purpose of taking up one dollar subscriptions for the purpose of building a pavilion sufficiently large to accommodate these immense audiences, which was included in a motion by Bro. Denton, and was put to the house and carried. The committee appointed were M. D. Kinsland, D. I. L. Smathers, and W. H. Hargrove.

The memorial committee reported the following names of those who have died and answered the last roll call since our last meeting at this place: Abel Stamey and wife, Riley Clouts, Taylor Harris, Mrs. Eliza Ford, Elisha Scott, George Scott, Mrs. Lucinda Cathey, Capt. T. B. Edmonston, David Vance, Mrs. Lilly Blalock.

The quartette sang a touching memorial tribute, and in closing the combined choir under the supervision of Mr. C. D. Fisher, sang a piece that was very much enjoyed by the audience.

Benediction by Rev. Willie Fincher.

Lively Chase

Some little excitement was cre-

Hack Hargrove published the *Canton Vindicator* weekly on Saturday, as evidenced by this clipping discovered hidden away in an old book. (Collection of the author.)

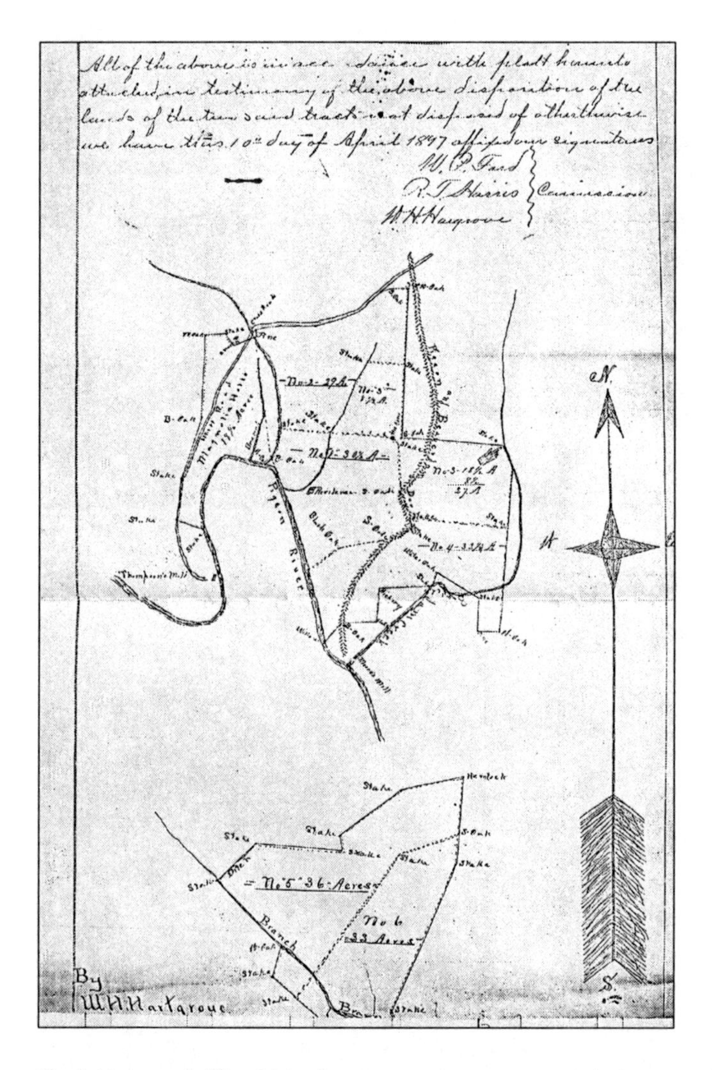

Hack Hargrove affixed his signature as a county commissioner and as the surveyor of record (employing variant spellings of his surname) to this 1897 map of a tract of land he surveyed and platted. (Collection of the author.)

in Haywood County at that time, so it can be surmised that he was devout in his politics and unafraid to express his political beliefs and thoughts.[34]

Hack apparently became involved in real estate sales as well, perhaps a natural outgrowth of his activities as surveyor. An advertisement prominently displayed in one of the early *Vindicator* editions promotes "W. H. Hargrove—Real Estate Agent." In these ads Hack offers great deals on lots in the booming mill town for $100 to $300, including generous financing terms.[35] Until the last year of his life Hack remained active and prominent in the Canton community and continued to engage in farming, publish newspapers, and serve as surveyor for the town of Canton. His professional occupations and interests were widespread, and undoubtedly old footprints leading to other ventures await discovery.

On April 20, 1909, Hack Hargrove, aged sixty-eight, departed the world of the living and his beautiful Pigeon Valley. After an extraordinary and productive life he was buried with Masonic honors at Bethel Cemetery. Hack's funeral was widely attended, with the notable exception of his eldest son, James (Jim) Hargrove, who had gone out West in search of gold and adventure. Jim was working mining claims near Beatty, Nevada, when he received a telegram from his brother, Dr. Theodore A. Hargrove, notifying him of their father's death. In response to this sad dispatch, Jim immediately wrote a letter back to Theodore. "[W]hat makes me feel so bad about it is that I didn't write to poor old Pa oftener," he wrote. "[H]e certainly had a hard time of it through life but if I was only as good a man as he always was I would feel that I was ready to go any time."

Many others surely wished the same—that they were only as good a man as Captain Hack Hargrove. Hack lived an extraordinary life filled with highs and lows, pain and joy, failure and success, and numerous accomplishments. In his obituaries published in local newspapers Hack was referred to as Canton's "first citizen," a "Useful Citizen," and a person that "has been closely identified with the affairs of the county, especially in the welfare and development of Canton."[36] No matter what his pursuits and vocations—Confederate soldier, farmer, teacher, politician, surveyor, railroad agent, or newspaperman—Captain Hack gave it his all and accomplished much. He was a useful citizen indeed.

Opposite: "The Cathey Mill" by Nettie Vance Penland, oil, 21½" × 15½", from Evelyn Coltman, *Legends, Tales & History of Cold Mountain,* books 3 and 4. (Painting from collection of Eula Rigdon; used by permission.)

4 Cathey's Mill

"Turn of meal" or "turn o' meal" was an expression the old-timers often used in referring to a person's successive turn, or opportunity. At the old gristmills "each man's corn was ground in turn—he waited his turn."[1] Of course one hardly ever hears this idiom used today, but back when William Hartgrove was a young boy growing up in Haywood County's Pigeon Valley he anxiously awaited the miller's pronouncement that it was his father's turn o' meal to have his corn ground. That would have been at Cathey's mill in Forks of Pigeon around about 1850. Located on the East Fork prong just above where the East and West forks of the Pigeon River are joined, Cathey's mill was owned by Colonel Joseph Cathey, a well-respected and prominent citizen in the area. Cathey also owned a general mercantile store situated nearby, and his two enterprises were the hub of the community in that day and were important centers of commerce for the Pigeon Valley settlers.

Any young boy would have been thrilled at the opportunity to go to the mill and see the marvelous workings of the huge water wheel

The first Cathey Mill at Forks of Pigeon was built in the 1840s by Colonel Joseph Cathey and Etheldred Blaylock. It burned down in 1869 and was replaced by the more substantial structure shown in this photo, which operated into the 1890s. (Collection of Charles Cathey.)

driving wooden-geared mechanisms and huge grinding stones inside. The colonel's facility was driven by a fourteen-foot water wheel and water diverted from the Pigeon River. The vertical wheel worked much like a turbine, made to turn by the force of water flowing under the wheel and striking blades mounted on the wheel's periphery. This undershot design, as it was called, was simpler to build than the overshot method by which the water is sluiced over the top of the wheel. Although the undershot wheel was less powerful, it was especially suited to conditions where the river bed was relatively flat. Moreover, it was the next best option when the difficulties of obtaining a source of water high enough to flow over the top of an overshot wheel could not be reasonably overcome.

Dred Blaylock is said to have built the mill for Colonel Cathey sometime in the 1840s while he was still a relatively young man—probably not yet thirty years old.[2] This native mechanic and builder, who later served as a lieutenant in the Confederate 25th Regiment North Carolina Infantry Troops, constructed a three-story building to house the milling machinery.[3] It is not clear how many sets of millstones were used with the operation. However, it is known that the gearing that transferred the energy and torque from the water wheel's main horizontal rotating axle to the vertical shafts that turned the heavy granite millstones was all hand crafted from wood. Certainly, it took the combination of Blaylock's mechanical and crafting genius and Cathey's clever intellect to conceive and construct this processing mill capable of grinding corn and other grain products grown in the region.

Drawn to the machinery of the mill with a boy's insatiable curiosity, the wide-eyed, youthful William would have taken in everything about the unfolding scene. He surely watched and listened to the miller bark directions to men unloading and hefting baskets of corn and wheat to the hoppers located above the sets of grinding stones. The miller was the boss of the mill's operation, and although it is not known for certain who William might have observed, it very well could have been John Man, or Mann, who is listed in the 1850 Haywood County census as a "miller" and enumerated directly below the immediate family of Joseph Cathey.

If young William could have followed John Mann inside, he would have seen the miller throw a lever to open a sluice gate and begin feeding the Hartgrove's corn through a hole in the top stone to fall between the groaning round millstones. With a practiced eye and trained ear, the miller set the gap between the top runner stone and the lower bed stone to grind the corn to the exact texture ordered by William's father. As the runner stone slowly turned against the stationary bed stone the shells of corn were sheared and ground between the hard stone surfaces into finer and finer particles. Grooves cut into the faces of the millstones facilitated the cutting action and movement of the ground meal outward, where it fell over the perimeter edge of the bed stone into a wooden vat enclosing the stones. Once collected in the vat, the meal spilled through the meal spout into waiting sacks below, where the farmer's treasure was captured.

After measuring out a portion of the meal in a toll dish, or toddick, to compensate the miller for his services, the father and son would have latched hold of their precious sack of meal and loaded it aboard whatever means of conveyance they employed on that particular day—wagon, sled, or the old mule. Before heading off for home, however, they may very well have stopped off at the store to pick up some vital necessity for the home. Cathey's store, located in the vicinity of the mill, was where the folk from the Forks of Pigeon area came to buy or barter for goods that could not be grown at home or were not easily crafted. As William's keen eyes perused the store's contents, he would have been overwhelmed by the exciting sights and aromas to be found there.

The counters and tables and floor were filled with all manner of goods, including farm tools, hand tools, hardware, rope, spices, coffee, produce, foodstuffs, flatware, silverware, colorful calico materials, clothing, hats, boots, and medicines. Hard and soft candies with wonderful fragrances and colors were also presented in great abundance to tease a youngster's senses. And, of course, there were always Cathey family members about that William knew and could visit and fool around with. He would in time marry Nancy Louisa Cathey, Colonel Cathey's granddaughter; and it would not be overly presumptuous to believe that he saw her as a toddler on occasion at the store as she played and entertained her grandfather's customers. Who can say what thoughts or sparks were initiated upon these first innocent encounters?

Also located in the store building was the Forks of Pigeon post office, where letters were received and posted. For a small fee, the colonel or one of his employees wrote letters for their customers whose literary skills were understandably lacking. Somewhere upon the grounds of the Cathey enterprises, too, William's uncles, Alfred Franklin and John Hartgrove, plied their blacksmith skills. Through their extraordinary abilities to shape iron over hot forges into useful implements and hardware, they provided a vital service for Colonel Cathey's customers and the community.

Eventually William would get the signal from his father that broke the strange spell which the store held over him, the dreaded look or nod of the head that told him it was time to go. Tired and hungry after a long day at the mill, William Hartgrove strode over to his father's side, and the two set out for home. Undoubtedly, racing through the youth's mind already were fervent hopes that the next turn o' meal at Cathey's would be a short time in coming.

Farmers living in the Forks of Pigeon area were accustomed to making long droves to distant markets in Greenville, South Carolina, and Augusta, Georgia. (Illustration by Elizabeth Cramer McClure from Ora Blackmun, *Western North Carolina, Its Mountains and Its People to 1880,* 1977. Used by permission.)

HACK HARGROVE'S
DROVE TO MARKET
1870

NORTH CAROLINA
Forks of Pigeon
Asheville
Greenville
SOUTH
CAROLINA
Augusta
GEORGIA

5 A Drove to Market

TODAY WE THINK NOTHING of hopping in our car and making a quick trip to the market. However, for our ancestors who settled the mountains of western North Carolina, a trip to the market was not such a simple proposition. My great-grandfather William "Hack" Hargrove made many journeys from his home in the Pigeon Valley down the Buncombe Turnpike to the distant markets of his day in Greenville, South Carolina, and Augusta, Georgia. Fortunately, he left behind some scribblings in an old notebook that give some insight into these annual market trips.[1] From Hack's accounts, other historical information, and our own imaginations it is possible to gain an appreciation for what those epic treks along the interstate highway of his day must have been like in the period immediately following the Civil War.

About 1827 the Buncombe Turnpike was completed, linking Greeneville, Tennessee, and Greenville, South Carolina. This wagon road passed through Asheville and served for more than fifty years

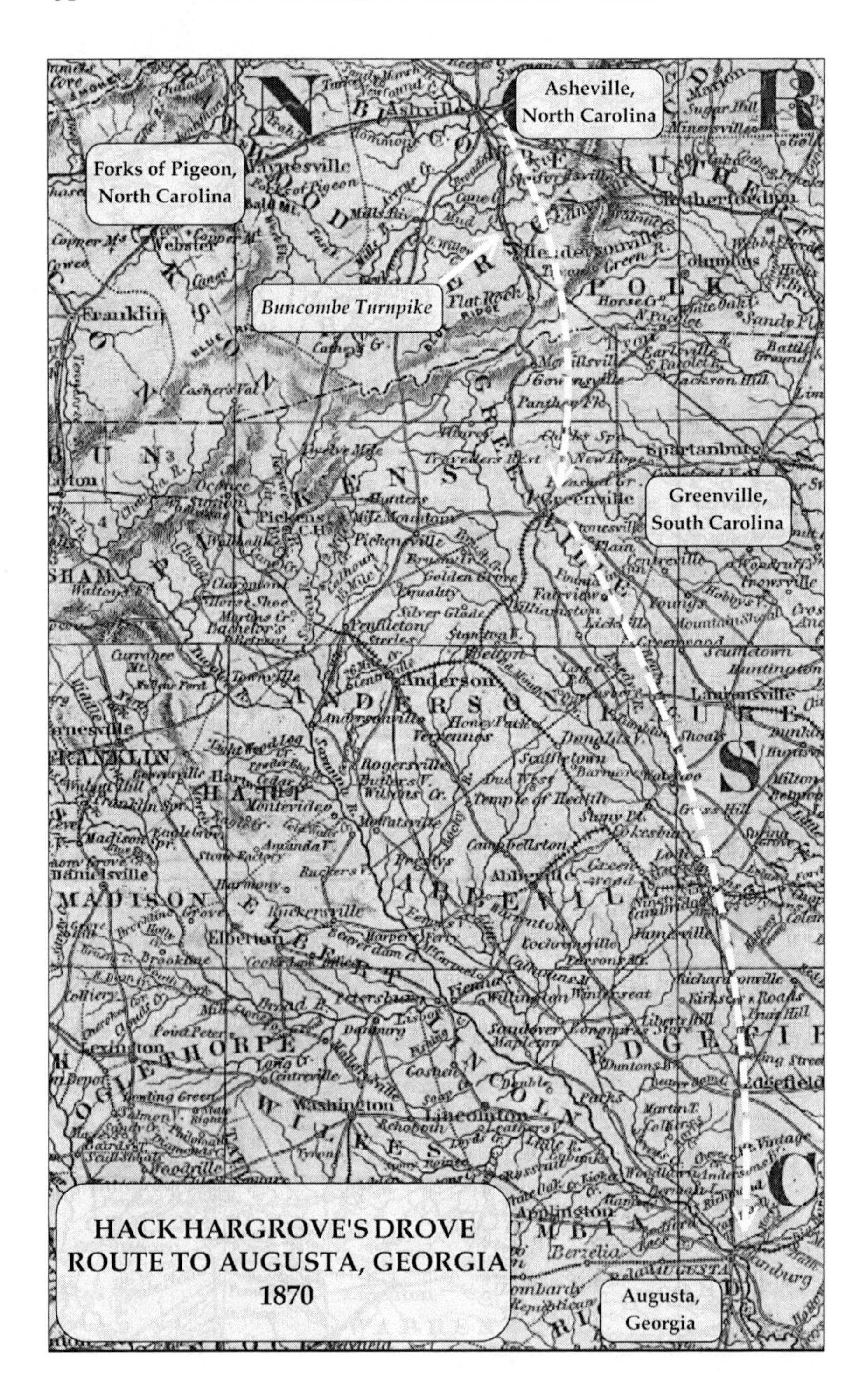
Asheville, North Carolina
Forks of Pigeon, North Carolina
Buncombe Turnpike
Greenville, South Carolina
Augusta, Georgia
HACK HARGROVE'S DROVE ROUTE TO AUGUSTA, GEORGIA 1870

as the primary artery of transportation for a majority of the populace of western North Carolina. It immediately opened up the mountains for trade to outsiders wishing to engage in commerce in a region hitherto barely accessible to wagon and stagecoach traffic. For local mountaineer farmers, this road provided the means by which their surplus farm crops and livestock could be transported and sold or bartered at distant lowland markets.[2]

Hack Hargrove used this fine road on numerous occasions to reach the markets in South Carolina and Georgia. He must have relished the opportunities as a teenager to accompany his father and neighbors on these adventures to faraway places. However, Hack's life was abruptly interrupted in 1861 by the Civil War, as were the lives of most young men throughout the South. Upon his return to the Pigeon Valley, after four horrific years of fighting with the 25th North Carolina Regiment to defend his homeland, "Captain" Hack recommenced his annual market treks down the Buncombe Turnpike. And when he did, he found a road in extreme disrepair and the conditions deplorable compared to the prewar state.

During the Civil War, both Confederate and Union Forces used the turnpike to move through the mountains on forays and a few limited strategic actions.[3] While the men of the South were consumed in fighting the war, roads, farms, and homesteads alike were much neglected during their absence. Sections of the turnpike south of Asheville that once had been corduroyed, or covered over with thick timber planks, were now beset with washouts and deep ruts, and the wood pavers for the most part had rotted away.

A drover and his team pass an inn along the Western Turnpike near Asheville. From Rebecca Harding Davis, "By-paths in the Mountains," *Harper's New Monthly Magazine* 61 (1880).

During the Reconstruction years following the war North Carolinians suffered through a sad state of affairs as they struggled to reestablish a government and determine the new societal role of freed slaves. The southern plantation economy was gone forever and the state, and entire South, was prostrate and bankrupt. Treasuries were depleted, and there was no money to repair the ruined infrastructure. For many years the Buncombe Turnpike, along with the state's eastern roads and railroads, was ignored.[4] Yet the turnpike remained as relevant and crucial to North Carolina's mountain economy as it had been prior to the war, if not more so. Even in its reduced state the road was still serviceable and useful to the mountain farmers and merchants—among them Hack Hargrove.

Upon the conclusion of hostilities between the alienated American states, Hack became a teacher and farmer. He and his bride, Nannie Cathey, made their home in the beautiful Pigeon Valley of Haywood County, where they raised corn and wheat crops. During those hard times currency was scarce, and farmers typically used a portion of their surplus corn and wheat yields to barter for goods and services locally. But the profits and returns for these valuable crops were more lucrative in Greenville or Augusta and offered such enticing rewards that Hack and his neighbors could justify the long, arduous trip there each fall after the crops were made and the animals fattened.

In 1870 Hack made a trip to the market in Augusta, Georgia (his usual destination), and made notes of daily expenses along the way.[5] According to the record he set out on November 17 and most likely was accompanied by an entourage of colleagues, neighbors, covered wagons loaded with grain products and apples, and an eclectic collection of livestock, including swine, cattle, and turkeys. From the Pigeon Valley Hack would have led his procession down a county roadway which generally followed the route of today's Highway 110, to the village of Pigeon River (now known as Canton).

Thereabouts they would have encountered the Western Turnpike, the primary east-west route through the western North Carolina mountains. Completed around 1850, this vital thoroughfare connected Asheville with Waynesville and points farther west, including

Webster, Franklin, Murphy, and beyond to Ducktown, Tennessee, and north Georgia.[6] From the small river hamlet of Pigeon River this turnpike snaked eastward through a gap in the Newfound Mountain Range and followed the course of Hominy Creek. It passed by John C. Smathers' roadside drovers' and stagecoach inn at Turnpike, located very near to the Buncombe-Haywood county line, and meandered through the areas today occupied by the communities of Candler and Enka. This route along Hominy Creek facilitated the passage of early pioneers into the Pigeon River drainage basin. Even earlier, it was used by General Griffith Rutherford in 1776 when he led a military force into the mountain fastnesses on a "scorched earth" campaign against the Cherokee Indians.

Beyond the present environs of Enka, the Western Turnpike continued in an easterly direction, running by the fashionable health resort hub of Sulfur Springs and along a route roughly approximating today's Sulfur Springs Road and Haywood Road before crossing the French Broad River at Sandy Bottom into Asheville. At that time Asheville, although considered the largest town in North Carolina's western mountains, was little more than a hamlet consisting of approximately 1,500 residents and a few dirt roads and paths.[7] Hack's notes indicate that on November 18 he paid a toll of fifty cents at Hominy Creek and the next day paid another toll of sixty-five cents at Sandy Bottom. Upon entering the Asheville area he would have rolled onto the Buncombe Turnpike and with a quick pop of the reins and a cry of "get-up" would have turned the team to the right and headed due south.

On November 19 Hack purchased corn and fodder for $1.40 at "King's," likely one of the first drovers' stations encountered along the Buncombe Turnpike and where he might have stopped for the night. Drovers' stations, or inns, were situated along the entire length of the Turnpike every few miles to accommodate the drovers, farmers, and their livestock. These stations were for many years veritable industries, procuring grain, produce, and hog's meat from local farmers and in turn selling these products to hordes of transient farmers moving their hard-won agrarian capital to the marketplace.

The records of the era reveal that literally hundreds of thousands of turkey, swine, and cattle were driven and coerced along the Turnpike annually. Large pens associated with the drovers' stations were used to corral the livestock overnight—with the exception of the turkeys. These unpredictable creatures usually found their own roosting accommodations in nearby trees. Corn and fodder purchased from the station proprietor or taken directly from the drovers' own wagons were fed to the animals each evening. Only after Hack's livestock and beasts of burden were properly nourished and cared for could he and his companions finally rest a spell and have their supper. The weary group would have happily joined in with other sojourners gulping down the innkeeper's bountiful meal of cooked vegetables, ham, and cornbread or biscuits slathered with molasses and churned butter. Milk and cider were consumed in huge quantities and, more likely than not, potent distilled spirits were available to those with a hankering for its peculiar effects. Surely, between mouthfuls and heaping helpings, the travelers would have shared tales about the adventures or mishaps of the day and anticipated the morrow's challenges on the next leg of the journey.

There would have been much discourse regarding a "soon start" the next morning in order to get out ahead of the other drovers. Hack and his cohorts would have tried to be the first out of the station so as to avoid the huge clouds of dust kicked up by herds of driven animals ahead of them on the road. Eventually, as the darkness and chill of the night closed in on the Pigeon Valley band, they would have looked for sleeping accommodations either on the inn floors or outdoors under the night sky and stars. Barring inclement weather, Hack—a hardened veteran and no stranger to nights on the ground—might have been inclined to take his rest with friends under the wagons and near their critters and "stuff."

A routine was soon established and repeated day after day for some sixteen days until the Augusta market destination was reached. Hack's notes affirm that he stopped at other drovers' stations along the way usually purchasing corn and fodder each night for the livestock. Leaving Asheville behind, the Buncombe Turnpike ran a mostly southward course passing through the villages of Hendersonville and Flat Rock and across the Green River, where Hack was obliged to pay another toll. At that point the road began a treacherous descent of the mountains through Butt Mountain Gap and Saluda Gap and after passing Traveler's Rest reached the Greenville area.

From Greenville, Hack had a choice of routes to complete the final leg of the journey to Augusta, Georgia, an important trade center located on the Savannah River. The maps of the period show more than one southward path leading toward Augusta, and there was even railroad service through the state's capital city of Columbia. Though better-drained and more gently sloping roads certainly facilitated this part of the journey, the caravan still faced another one hundred miles of slogging in the autumn chill. Hack wrote in the little notebook he carried that he reached the river town of Augusta, Georgia, on December 3, about nine days after leaving Greenville.

Finally, after eighteen days of grueling conditions and tedious plodding along the Buncombe Turnpike and the sandy-clay roads of South Carolina, the little group of mountaineers arrived at their market destination of Augusta. Hack would've wasted little time in selling the livestock and grain for rare United States legal tender or bartering it for commodities that could not be produced at home such as sugar, salt, coffee, and cloth. Once done with the bargaining and haggling and familiar with the strange sights and sounds of the bustling river town, the group would have loaded up and headed back for the hills. Though weary, dirty, and possibly a trifle homesick, the mountaineers would surely have been in higher spirits on the return trip to the Pigeon Valley. They had pockets full of money, their wagons were loaded with precious foreign goods, and, thank the Lord, they no longer had to contend with those smelly hogs and rascally turkeys.

Hack arrived back in the Pigeon Valley on December 17, a full month after starting out for Augusta. No mention is made in his notes of observing the Thanksgiving holiday that Abraham Lincoln had made official just a few years before, nor of any turkeys being sacrificed for the occasion. On the return journey Hack would have parted with some of his hard-earned currency to pay the toll operators and drovers' station proprietors for debts incurred on the outward leg of the journey. And apparently Hack's wagon broke down along the steep climb back up into the mountains just below the Saluda Gap, for he noted in his journal a payment of $4.00 for a new axle tree.

No matter—it would have taken more than a broken-down wagon to dampen Hack Hargrove's spirits on that homeward stretch, because someone very special was waiting for him back in the Valley. Not Nannie, who certainly would be relieved and proud to see her husband home safe and sound. That special "someone" was little James Burton Hargrove, the couple's first child, born just three weeks before Hack departed for Augusta. Hack would have been eager to see how their son had grown during his absence.

My great-grandfather continued to make these trips to the lowland markets every fall or winter. And incredible as it may sound, in 1875 Hack and his brother-in-law, James Webster Cathey, had the gumption and stamina to make two trips to the market. But only a few years after that remarkable feat the long market droves along the Buncombe Turnpike would no longer be necessary. With the coming of the Western North Carolina Railroad to Asheville in 1880, to Pigeon River in 1882, and to regions farther west soon after, the farmers were then able to use this more efficient means of transportation to access the markets beyond the mountains.

Today it is difficult to contemplate taking an entire month to go to the market. However, our mountaineer ancestors did just that each year after their crops were made and the weather turned cool and crisp. Their livelihood and existence depended on it. Extended absences from family and friends and long, tortuous, and sometimes hazardous market journeys were a way of life, and were tolerated for generations until the railroad at last penetrated into the remote mountain regions.

Hack Hargrove lived to see the day that he need not bid farewell each fall to Nannie and their brood. Not only did he embrace the new mode of transportation on rails, he obtained employment with the Western North Carolina Railroad Company as their first agent at Pigeon River in 1882. Hack surely would have been pleased at not having to make those long market droves down the Buncombe Turnpike—and not having to fool with those danged independent turkeys.

Opposite: "The Old Home Place," watercolor by Jo Ridge Kelley, 2002. Used by permission.

6 Spring: A Time of Hope

Winters in the southern Appalachian highlands were harsh and sometimes cruel to the early settlers of yesteryear, especially to the brave pioneers who settled Haywood County's Pigeon River Valley and nearby ridges and coves some two hundred years ago. By the time spring finally arrived these hardy people were weary of the cold and snow and ice and of the close confines of small, dimly lit cabins. The advent of spring buoyed their hopes and spirits and presented to the families an opportunity to rejuvenate the Valley and resume agrarian pursuits that provided for creature sustenance, comfort, and pleasure.

Spring was certainly a time for hard work; but it was work that men, women, and children alike had been planning and contemplating all winter long. Their exertions and toils toward plowing and planting the fields, though tremendously tiring to the body, provided a sense of fulfillment and accomplishment. And not only was the work good for their souls, it was a means by which independent families could demonstrate to neighbors and the entire community their worth, their industry, and their ability to grow and make things and provide for themselves.

Spring in the Pigeon Valley was indeed a time for the mountain folk to thaw out and come alive again. Travel back in time with me and behold the sights and smells of springtime, when . . .

- *March winds gusting cold from the mountain peaks prolong memories of a wearisome winter and dim eager thoughts of warmer weather to come*

- *lingering snow hiding in the shadows gradually melts away and frost's bite retreats to the highest ridges and peaks*

- *the rhododendrons, huddling amidst the mountain laurel alongside streams and across ridges, slowly unfurl their clinched leaves and stretch thawing limbs to capture the warmth*

- *farmers in the fields trudge and steer crude plows behind old mules that still wear winter's shaggy growth*

- *the earthy smell of the rich bottom loam and the scrabble of the ridges permeates everywhere, as restless farmers turn fields that have lain silent through winter's harsh spell*

- *ravenous bears emerge from their winter slumber in search of nourishment and nature's offerings*

• fierce March winds that roar and sweep down into the Valley are finally tamed by April's caressing rains and gentle breezes

• the Master's canvas of highlands and deep valleys gradually sheds its heavy winter cloak of gray and brown and dons a verdant green veil splashed with the white brushstrokes of flowering dogwoods and serviceberry

• the keen senses of the mountain folk suffer a confused blend of pungent wild onion odors and pleasing aromas of blossoming trees that pervade the Valley

• busy brooms fashioned from corn husks make the dirt and dust fly and children to seek safe haven, as mountaineer women rid their cabins of winter's accumulations

• birds of the mountain habit, such as the proud robins with their puffed orange breasts and the finicky crested blue jays, announce their return by filling the air once again with squawking, chirping, and singing

• the rays of the April sun inspire the plowmen in the fields and warm not only determined faces and stout backs but heavy hearts as well

• children liberate their feet and toes from heavy brogans and, oblivious to prickly thorns, enjoy the sensation of cool, soft earth and icy creek waters

• *the tiny white petals of the toothwort and bloodroot and the red, bell-shaped blossoms of the columbine lead a parade of wildflowers anxiously poking through the lush forest undercover*

• *the mountainsides are set ablaze with eruptions of bright orange blossoms from the flame azalea*

• *the fires of the blooming azalea are finally extinguished by waves of scarlet and lavender rhododendron washing across the hills*

• *fruit trees budding and bursting into bloom portend delightful pies, jellies, and butters to come, and delicious ciders to quench the thirst and steady the nerves*

• *entire families methodically roam plowed fields, poking and placing and stomping in an annual ritual designed to give life to their precious seeds and, in turn, nourish their very own needs*

• *speckled trout awaken from their winter dormancy, frantically rising and feasting on hatching mayflies afloat on the swift water's surface*

• *pioneer women and young'uns roam the fields and woods in search of wild salad greens, bringing home a delicious mess of fresh creases, poke, or wild lettuce*

• frightened sheep grudgingly sacrifice heavy winter wool coats to be spun and wrought by a woman's skilled hands into cherished clothes and coverlets for her family

• mountaineers congregate in small groups and little churches to worship at Easter time, and celebrate the rebirth of their land and the resurrection of their Savior

• the sun, reaching higher and higher into the sky, drowns out winter's despair and gloom and floods the land with its vernal rays of rejuvenation, birth, and hope.

Spring, the season of eternal hope, inspired our ancestors year after year. Springtime in the Pigeon Valley many years ago marked the end of shortened days and the beginning of renewal and birth for the land, nature, and humankind alike—as it still does today.

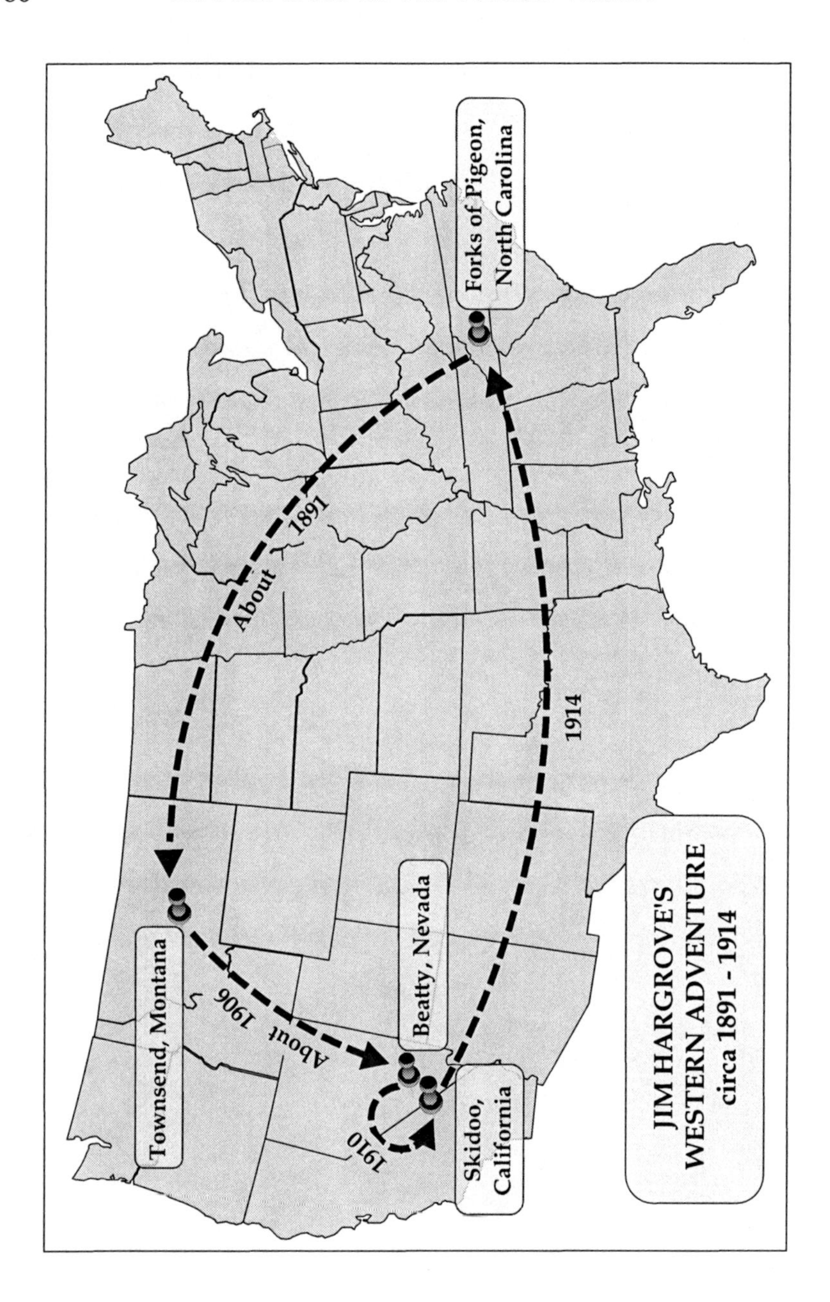

Opposite: James Burton (Jim) Hargrove in front of his Pigeon Valley farmhouse. (Collection of the author.)

7 Jim Hargrove's Western Adventure
A Quest for Gold in the Old West

I HAVE HEARD MANY TIMES THE ACCOUNT of how my grandfather escaped the mountains of western North Carolina as a young man to seek his fortune in gold. Aunt Nannie, my mother's sister, told the story best—or at least my brother and I thought so. You see, she would always end her Granddaddy Hargrove stories by reaching into the depths of an antique oak sideboard in her kitchen and retrieving a glass jar full of gold dust. Nannie allowed how her father had mined this gold and brought it back from the Old West. Imagine our excitement—imagine how our eyes must have lit up, as we gingerly held that jar of gold close to our faces and carefully inspected the yellow grains inside. That was half a century ago, but that jar of gold still glistens in my mind.

James (Jim) Burton Hargrove married and started a family later than most. He was already well past his fortieth birthday when he returned from his western gold-mining adventure and married my grandmother, Maggie Hazeltine Shook Evans. By all accounts, he was a loving, soft-spoken, and devoted husband to Maggie and a kindly and caring father to his daughters Lois Evans, Nannie, Ellen, Mildred and Jimmie Hargrove (my mother), and his son, Roy Evans. Jim was a simple farmer and raised corn and tobacco crops on fertile bottomland abutting the Pigeon River in Haywood County. Although my grandfather often read the Bible and theological works and was very thoughtful and respectful on the subject, I believe he was more devoted to his family than to religion.

But then again, I never knew my grandfather. He died thirteen years before I was born and has always been something of a mystery to me. A cherished picture of him in my office captures a thin, elderly man stoically posed in overalls, a suit coat, and a felt fedora with a center crease along the top. This image of a mountaineer farmer, not a gold miner, is the one that I envision when thinking of my grandfather. And that's where the mystery begins. What was the real story behind that jar of gold dust and its discoverer?

James Hargrove's Early Years

James Burton Hargrove was born in 1870 in Haywood County, North Carolina, in an area known at the time as Forks of Pigeon and today as the Pigeon Valley or simply Bethel. His father was William Harrison Hargrove, the farmer, war veteran, and civil servant local folk respectfully called Captain Hack.

James Hargrove's early years were undoubtedly spent like those of most other boys of his era—primarily farming, and going to school between growing seasons. He would surely have worked alongside his father and brothers planting and harvesting the crops, taking care of the livestock, hauling crops to the markets and mill, chopping firewood, fetching water, and engaging in all manner of essential tasks. And Nannie, who was regularly adding babies to the Hargrove clan every couple of years, would have looked for James to lend her assistance. Her familial duties would have included not only caring for the youngsters and cooking, but also cleaning, keeping the critters out of the house, tending the vegetable garden, and making soap, butter, and clothes for the family. Young James would have reluctantly helped with these chores. Yet he would have the chance to be close to his mother and to gain her confidence and insight into matters large and small. It is easy to imagine them chatting away over the whirring sound of the spinning wheel or the noisy clacking of a loom as Nannie busily worked in their dimly lit cabin.

After the crops were made and put away or hauled to the mill or market, James could take advantage of the book-learning opportunities available in the Valley. He likely attended Bethel school for at least a year or two to learn to read, write, and cipher. Although the schoolhouse would have been a short ride away from his parents' farm by horseback or wagon, I suspect that young James walked to school most of the time, as Hack probably owned only one horse or mule, which he would have needed himself.

When James's younger sister, Florence, came of schooling age, Captain Hack must have thought less favorably about that long walk to the Bethel schoolhouse. In 1880, or thereabouts, he and the Rhodarmers, their neighbors, organized and built a combination church and schoolhouse and named it Piney Grove.

The Piney Grove school had a fireplace and was furnished with rough wood-slab seats propped up with peg legs. On these the children sat, resting their books on their laps, as they studied and took turns warming their feet at the fire.[1] The new schoolhouse was nestled in a pretty little cove (known today as Stamey Cove) on the opposite side of the ridge where Hack had constructed his house. Undoubtedly the youthful Hargrove students rejoiced at the much shorter walk to their new school. In addition to the formal schooling at Bethel and Piney Grove schools, Hack would have supplemented James's education by personally tutoring and coaching his son. After all, Hack was a learned man for his time, who after returning from the Civil War had himself taught at the Chinquapin Grove and Bethel schoolhouses.

There were many aspects of rural Appalachian farm life in the 1870s and 1880s that would have introduced happiness and pleasure into a young man's life. "Preachings" and "singings" at the Methodist churches every Sunday not only helped to shape James's spiritual and moral character but would have provided social opportunities to mingle with neighbors and friends. Family gatherings, quilting bees, corn huskings, hoedowns, and the like also provided chances to interact with the community. Welcome diversions from the routine would have included fishing and hunting, and, of course, swimming in the cold waters of the Pigeon River on withering, hot summer afternoons.

Most assuredly, James did not pass up many opportunities to tag along with Hack on trips over to the Cathey/Blaylock mill and general store.[2] There he could watch the miller at his work or just eavesdrop on the men folk as they chewed and spat tobacco, whittling knives in hand, and discussed politics, weather, fertilizers, seed, and such. And eventually, as James grew into his teen years, he would have been a keen participant in these informal gatherings, absorbing the knowledge and wisdom of his neighbors and keeping up with the latest farming practices and news.

According to the 1880 U.S. census records there were eight persons residing in Captain Hack's household that year. In addition to James, who would have been ten years old, and his parents, there were sister Florence, age seven, and brothers Joseph, six, Theodore, three, and Walter, less than one year old. A thirty-five-year old white woman named Nancy West, whose occupation is listed as "servant," is enumerated with the household. Nothing is now known of the particular circumstances in which she came to live among them.

Sadly, in 1883 at the young age of thirty-four, Nannie Cathey passed away for reasons that escape us today. The mourning Hargrove family would have suffered a lengthy struggle to regain a normalcy and balance in their lives, and Hack, especially, would have been under a tremendous strain. He alone was left to raise the children, although certainly he would have relied heavily on the support of his mother, Ellen, or mother-in-law Lucinda Moore Cathey, and possibly Nancy West. Thirteen-year-old James would undoubtedly have had to step up and play a larger and more significant role around the farm and in caring for his younger siblings.

Over the next several years James would have to be at times a father to Theodore and Walter, a big brother to Joe and Florence, and the eldest son in charge of the farm while Hack was away. It was a period when Hack was extremely busy with various occupational pursuits and civic service, working as an agent for the Western North Carolina Railroad and serving on the county board of commissioners and board of education as well as representing Haywood County in the State Legislature. His duties pulled him away from the family on a frequent basis and sometimes for lengthy stretches of time. During these absences James and younger brother Joe surely had to fill the void and take care of the children and the farm chores.

As James matured and grew into his late teen years, folks who knew him well began to call him Jim. It is not evident whether Jim, at twenty years of age, was still living with his family in 1890 or had already struck out on his own. Lacking census data for that year (U.S. census records for 1890 were subsequently destroyed in a fire) or other family records from the period to reveal his whereabouts, we cannot establish with specificity when he removed from the Pigeon Valley. But leave he did—and family members of later generations have puzzled over the timing and motives for his departure.

Family lore—likely embroidered—has it that Jim and another young buck of the community got crosswise with each other, leading first to a tussle and then to a more serious affair. During this struggle, the legend allows, Jim grabbed a rock and hit the other fellow about the head with it, knocking him senseless to the ground. Fearing that he had killed the man, Jim fled from the scene and kept running until the Rocky Mountains got in his way.[3] There is a slight chance that this tale has some basis in fact. It is more likely that Jim left the mountains either because of some familial difficulty, of which there is no hard evidence, or simply because of his natural yearnings and instincts for adventure and independence. But one factor, even stronger, may in fact have enticed him to leave his mountain roots for the faraway frontier state of Montana.

Townsend, Montana

It appears that Jim vacated the western North Carolina mountains sometime around 1891, when he was twenty-one years old. U.S. census data for the year 1900 enumerates James Hargrove and about twenty other "boarders" living in a boarding house in Townsend, Montana. The record identifies his profession, like that of several fellow tenants, as "quartz miner." The boarders hailed from all parts of the country and even from England, Ireland, Sweden, and Germany. Their varied occupations included telegraph operator, teamster, bartender, carpenter, painter, chemist, publisher, salesman, cook, and head waiter. All were in some way tied to the mining economy of the surrounding communities spawned by the Gold Rush, or to the Northern Pacific Railroad, which had just come to that frontier region. Although in 1900 Townsend had been in existence for only about seven years, the gold was pretty well played out in the area, the town's population was dwindling, and the mines were already closing one by one.

But Jim Hargrove had a strong justification for settling and working in the region, as he had close kin nearby. Several Hargroves had removed from Haywood County in 1880 to start their lives over again in what was then the Territory of Montana (Montana did not become a state until 1889), where land was inexpensive and grasslands abundant. His great-uncle Alfred Franklin Hargrove and family had joined up with a group of some forty-three related persons from Haywood County and made the trek to Montana by railroad and wagon train. Records show that they left on May 1, 1880, and traveled by train to Corrinne, Utah, near Salt Lake City. There they bought horses and wagons and journeyed in a wagon train through Virginia City, Radersburg, Diamond, and Helena to White Sulfur Springs, Montana, arriving on June 15, 1880. Alfred and his family and many of the other Haywood County migrants put down roots in nearby Townsend, Montana, and the surrounding area.[4]

Jim would have known all of these Hargroves very well. His first cousin who traveled with this group, Thomas Franklin Hargrove, was the same age as Jim, and they certainly would have been fast friends during their boyhood days. Jim likely heard grand stories of this Montana country from his father, and he must have fancied those tales of cowboying and prospecting for gold. Sometime around his twentieth birthday, or shortly after, when he was in the prime of life and filled with youthful vigor, strength, and confidence, Jim decided it was high time to pursue his dreams. (His own father had been only twenty when he marched off to war in 1861.) And he chased these dreams to the new state of Montana, where Great-Uncle Alfred and Cousin Thomas were living. It is probable that Jim reunited and lived with these close Hargrove relations for a year or more until he got comfortably situated and learned the mining trade. His natural penchant for risk and adventure would have made him easily susceptible to the "gold fever" epidemic that prevailed throughout the West and infected thousands of young men just like him.

Eventually Jim took up his new occupation, as the census shows, but there are no clues to reveal when he actually became a miner or how successful his prospecting trade might have been. For the most part these hard-rock quartz miners would try to find land with enough evidence of gold to file a claim and obtain the rights to mine it. Or they would lease ore-bearing ground from mining companies or other claim holders who held the mineral rights. If successful in getting hold of some good ground, the miners would proceed to use whatever equipment they had available and could afford—picks, hammers, shovels, sacks, buckets, wheelbarrows, pneumatic drills—to excavate the quartz rock with the gold inside. Once this quartz rock, or ore, was extracted the miners would either sell it to the mining companies or pay the companies to "stamp" or crush their ore and extract the gold for them. Mining was not work for the faint of heart and weak of body. It required strength, endurance, persistence, and, most important, good luck.[5] The fact that Jim Hargrove pursued his mining obsession for so many years indicates that he possessed all of these qualities and that he was at least moderately successful in his efforts.

Sometime before early 1907 Jim probably surmised that the worked-out mines around Townsend were too lean and unproductive and that he might try his lot elsewhere. He had resided and worked in the Townsend area for many years and it would not have been easy to again leave all his relations and friends behind. But an adventurous spirit and persistent fever for gold lured him away from family and led him on a long journey through the mountains of Idaho to Utah's Salt Lake City. From there it was only a short jump to the extreme southwestern tip of Nevada, where the Bullfrog Mining District beckoned and new gold discoveries and fortunes were being made every day.

Beatty, Nevada

In 1907 Beatty, Nevada, was a small hard-rock mining community located near the California state line and close to Death Valley. It was established in 1905 and was organized along with other nearby gold-mining communities such as Rhyolite, Gold Center, and Bullfrog into the Bullfrog Mining District. Most of these small towns that suddenly sprouted around the gold mines quickly disappeared after the gold played out. The only town from the district that survives today is Beatty, which still serves as an important gateway to Death Valley, and is the first community of size north of Las Vegas.[6] Jim Hargrove was lured to Beatty by the prospects of finding gold there, and he ended up working in and around that region from 1907 until June 1910.

Records reveal that as early as April 1907 Jim worked hard-rock mines approximately nine miles east of Beatty. He and a partner, Jim Biddlesome, filed at least six claims with the Bullfrog Mining District for ground on the slopes of Bare Mountain where they had found evidence of gold and staked out their claims. The first of these was filed in May 1907 and the last in February 1908. Each colorfully titled claim—Golden Queen, Golden Queen No. 1, Southern, Jackass No. 3, Corsair, and Clipper No. 4—asserts rights to 1,500 linear feet along the course of the mineral-bearing ledge, lode, or vein. The claims would occupy the attention and energies of Jim and his friend Biddlesome for approximately three years.[7]

In July 1908, during his tenure in the Beatty area, Jim joined the Fraternal Order of Eagles lodge. Relatively new at the time, the organization was founded in 1898 in Seattle, Washington, and quickly grew all across the country. The order was unique in its concept of brotherhood, and its early success has been attributed to the establishment of a sick and funeral benefit along with provisions for a physician and other amenities. These benefits would have been important to Jim, whose gold mining trade was extremely difficult and hazardous. The social aspect of the order, too, was likely attractive to single men like Jim who were far from kin and friends. The records show that Jim was a good dues-paying member of the Eagles until he vacated Beatty.

It is more than just another family rumor that Jim was partial to gambling. During slow periods between leases, or when the weather was too bad for mining work, Jim likely frequented the saloons of Beatty or nearby Flourine or other towns to play poker and other card games of chance. My mother used to tell how her father had won and lost entire gold mines playing poker. He swore to her, too, that he knew exactly where the fabled Lost Dutchman's Mine was

F.O.E. OFFICIAL RECEIPT F.O.E.

No 38 Fraternal Order of Eagles

190

This Certifies that Brother Jas B. Hargrave

Has Paid to BEATTY AERIE No. 1852 F.O.E.

of State of NEV

the sum of Six Dollars

Dues $6

Initiation

Fines & Ass'ts

Card

Total $6

in full for all Charges to date and Dues to

Seal

Secretary

F.O.E. OFFICIAL RECEIPT F.O.E.

INDEPENDENT ORDER OF ODD FELLOWS

$ 12.00 Townsend, Mont., Oct 28 1912

This Certifies that Jas B. Hargrove

whose signature appears in the margin hereof

Has paid To NORTH STAR Lodge No. 19 I.O.O.F.

of Townsend, Jurisdiction of Montana,

the sum of Twelve Dollars

OFFICIAL CERTIFICATE

in full for all charges to Dec 1912

Seal Except assessments levied after the date of this certificate

Noble Grand Secretary

Dues receipts indicate that Jim Hargrove belonged to two fraternal organizations during his time out West, the Order of the Odd Fellows and the Order of the Eagles. (Collection of the author.)

located. Incredible as it sounded to me then, and now for that matter, my guess is that Jim may actually have won or lost a mining claim or two at the gambling tables. But that Lost Dutchman's Mine is still lost, and I have serious doubts that Jim Hargrove had a fix on its whereabouts.

It was during the time that Jim was working in and around Beatty that his father, Hack, passed away back in the Pigeon Valley, on April 20, 1909. Jim's brother, Dr. Theodore A. Hargrove, notified him immediately by telegram. Jim responded by letter. "[W]hat makes me feel so bad about it is that I didn't write to poor old Pa oftener," he wrote. "[H]e certainly had a hard time of it through life but if I was only as good a man as he always was I would feel that I was ready to go any time." [8]

Jim was obviously saddened and hurt with the news of his dad's passing. The words he wrote back to Theodore are not only a testament to the kind of man Hack Hargrove was but manifestly demonstrate the love, affection, and respect of a son for his father. No presumption will be made regarding the feelings of sorrow and loneliness that Jim must have felt during this period. Removed from family by thousands of miles and now from his father forever, Jim may well have found Hack's passing an awakening of sorts that may have agitated longings for home, family, and the Pigeon Valley.

After three or four years of working their mining claims in the surrounds of Beatty, Jim and his partner presumably ran out of productive ground to dig. They plainly were able to stay ahead of expenses and subsist, but their excruciating toils apparently bore little of the yellow treasure they sought. The records do not indicate that the two miners struck it rich or discovered Bare Mountain's mother lode. What they do reveal is that the mountaineer prospector from

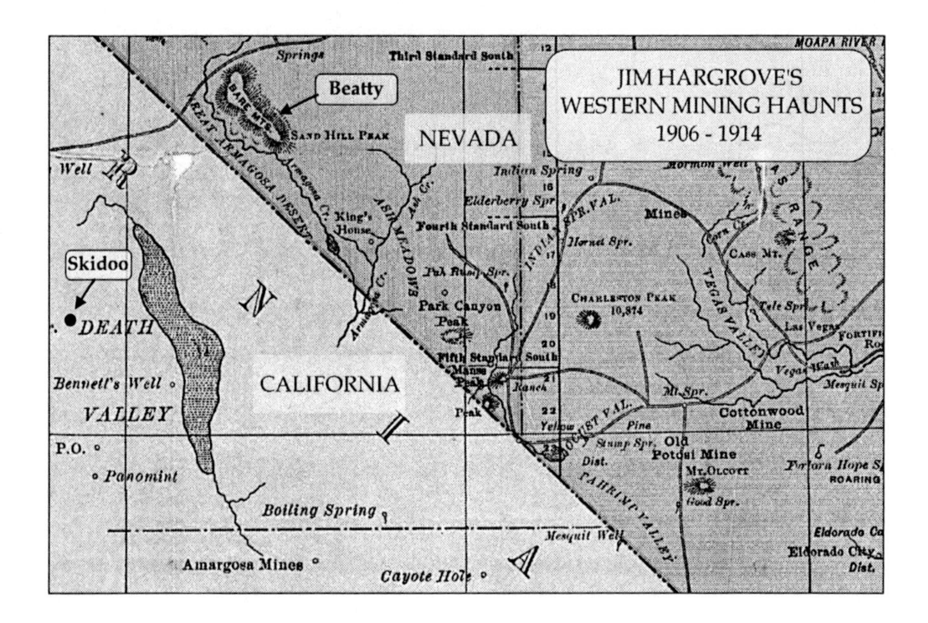

the Carolina highlands, still under the influence of an overpowering compulsion to find gold, pulled up stakes in the Nevada hills and struck out to find his fortune in the barren mountains bordering California's Death Valley.

Skidoo, California

Some forty miles' distance from Beatty, across the Nevada–California state line and just beyond Death Valley in the mountains along its western edge, was another upstart mining community, Skidoo, California. To reach it from Beatty, Jim would have crossed the Armagosa Desert, traversed the Grapevine Mountains, ventured across Death Valley itself, and then climbed up to the Skidoo gold digs located high in the Panamint Mountains some 5,600 feet above sea level. One can easily imagine a difficult and tortuous journey by pack mule, wagon, or stagecoach across the infamous Death Valley. This barren, waterless desert, of Borax "20-mule team" fame, is situated below sea level and has the harshest and most inhospitable environment in the country. Jim had surely never encountered terrain such as this—desolate, wild, hostile and seemingly isolated from the rest of the world—and certainly would have contemplated the striking disparity of such environs with the lush green mountains of North Carolina.

Skidoo was founded about 1906 after two lucky prospectors accidentally found a bit of gold and traced it back to the lode in the Panamint Mountains. The Skidoo Mining Company proceeded to buy all the claims in the area. A fifteen-stamp mill was soon constructed to process the ore and the mining company began to build a twenty-three-mile long water pipeline to provide the driving force for the mill's machinery. Considered a cut above most mining towns, Skidoo had a newspaper, a school, a bank, a brothel, saloons, a post office, restaurants, a physician, lawyers, and even a telephone service. There were also stores offering mining equipment, hardware, clothing, dry goods, and groceries. In April 1907 Skidoo had 130 homes and businesses of frame, wood, and iron. A phone line had been completed to Rhyolite, permitting outside communication. In November 1907, the pipeline was completed and water flowed into Skidoo. By the fall of 1908 the town's population had reached 700, but mining activity had slowed tremendously due to the scarcity of mills in the area. Mining ebbed and flowed in Skidoo over the next several years, and in September 1917 the rich vein was played out and the mine closed down for the last time.

Skidoo gained notoriety in 1908 as the site of the only hanging to take place in Death Valley. Hootch Simpson, a saloon owner who had fallen on hard times, tried to rob the bank, was foiled in the attempt, and later went back and killed the owner of the store in which the bank was located. During the night the townspeople hanged Hootch. According to legend, he was hanged twice—the second occurrence staged to accommodate news photographers who missed the first hanging.[9] This boomtown would not have been most people's first choice of a place to live and work, but for some unfathomable reason it was the place to which my grandfather gravitated and settled for a brief spell as he pursued an obsession for gold and adventure.

When Jim arrived in Skidoo in June 1910 the peak gold-producing period was over, but there was still some gold to be found. Undoubtedly one of the first things he did was to stop by the Skidoo Trading Company and stock up on supplies. A 1913 account sheet in Jim's name from the store shows that he made purchases on nine different days during the month of February. He bought food staples: spuds, onions, bacon, flour, lard, baking powder, salt, pepper, beans, milk, sugar, coffee, syrup, eggs, corn, and chow chow. He also bought several plugs of Star tobacco, soap, candles, toothpicks, strawberries, B. [butter] jelly, persimmons, dried apricots, butter, coal, and coal oil. The bill at the end of the month totaled twenty-nine dollars.[10]

Of course the coal oil, or kerosene, would have been used to fuel lamps and light Jim's way into the mines as he dug and blasted and traced the narrow veins of gold back into the mountainsides. Because of its high elevation above sea level Skidoo could get extremely cold in the winter months, and it was always a challenge for the mining company to keep their water pipeline from freezing up. The coal Jim purchased would have fueled a stove to keep his small living quarters warm and comfortable.

Records of this period show that while in Skidoo Jim was paying dues to the Independent Order of Odd Fellows back in Townsend, Montana. One receipt for his dues includes an envelope postmarked in Townsend and mailed to James B. Hargrove, Esq., in Skidoo.[11] It is probable that Jim joined this fraternal organization while living in Townsend, although no evidence of that fact has been uncovered. The Odd Fellows was another benevolent and social society, similar to the Fraternal Order of Eagles, whose primary aim was to provide its members with aid during periods of illness, unemployment, or other misfortunes. Jim's penchant for these fraternal organizations may have stemmed from an appreciation of the beneficiary aspects more than anything else.

The record of Jim's activity in Skidoo is fairly silent until 1912. Enumerators for the 1910 census records somehow missed him—no matches for Hargroves (including similar spellings) born in North Carolina and of Jim's age can be found anywhere in the country. But he certainly was residing in Skidoo by July 1910, when documents show that he joined the Skidoo Miners Union No. 211.[12] Also, dues receipts from the Odd Fellows beginning in June 1910 and running through May 1913 were being mailed to him in Skidoo. Based on these scant records it is evident that Jim must have resided and

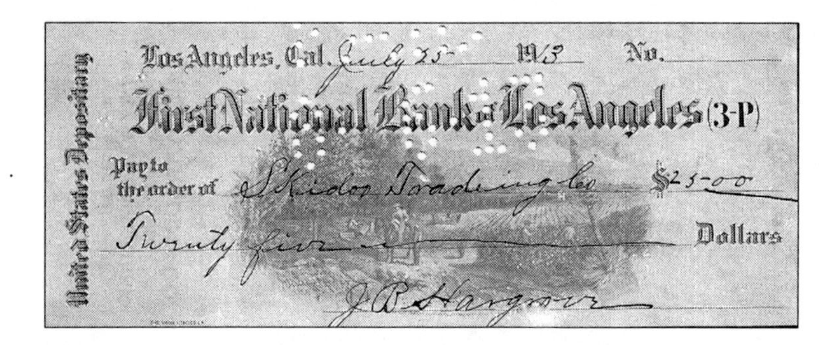

Los Angeles, Cal. July 25 1913 No.

First National Bank of Los Angeles (3-P)

Pay to the order of Skidoo Trading Co $25-00

Twenty five Dollars

J B Hargrove

United States Depositary

In Skidoo, California, Jim Hargrove regularly purchased supplies from the Skidoo Trading Company (below). To pay down his account at the mercantile store in July 1913, as shown in the cashed check above, he drew on funds held in the First National Bank of Los Angeles. (Collection of the author.)

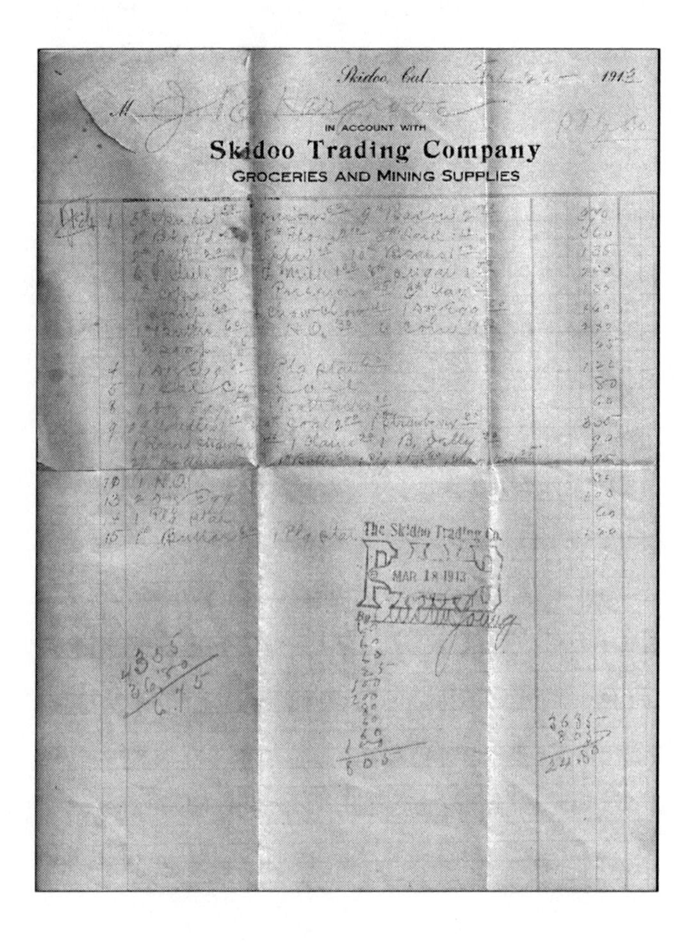

Skidoo, Cal. 1913

M J B Hargrove

IN ACCOUNT WITH

Skidoo Trading Company

GROCERIES AND MINING SUPPLIES

The Skidoo Trading Co.

PAID

MAR 18 1913

diligently pursued his gold-mining passion in Skidoo from about June 1910 until at least 1913.

Jim's extant financial records show that, while he never became wealthy, he had adequate means for his living and his business ventures. During his stint at Skidoo, Jim would occasionally have visited Los Angeles, California, a day's train and stagecoach ride away. A checkbook from the First National Bank of Los Angeles shows an opening balance of $1,967.66 in an account opened in Los Angeles on October 5, 1912. From this date until the last check was written on November 29, 1913, Jim drew regularly from the account with no evidence of deposits being made. Many of the checks were written to "self" and for cash. A total of seven checks were written to the Skidoo Trading Company spaced one to two months apart.[12]

Jim would likely have maintained an account at the local bank in Skidoo as well. Although it is not obvious how Jim managed his financial concerns, he would have either sold his ore to the company in exchange for U.S. currency or gold, or would have paid the company to process his gold. One way or the other, Jim would have certainly needed the relative security of the bank's vault to protect his currency and gold.

An examination of Jim's checking activities and the bank stamps on the backs of the cashed checks suggest that his mining activities were slowing down in the latter part of 1913. There is only one check to the Skidoo Trading Company after July 1913, and it appears that some of the checks written after July of that year were tendered to settle accounts. Also, in November 1913 one check was received and stamped in Bakersville, California (an intermediate stop on the train route from Skidoo to Los Angeles) and another drawn and cashed in Los Angeles. It appears that in November 1913 Jim was in Los Angeles, and not in Skidoo mining.

Two surviving hand-written letters from friends offer an insight into his activities during this time frame, and into the gold mining business. One correspondent, whose name has been lost, wrote to Jim in Beatty, Nevada, from Skidoo on December 15.

> Friend Jim:
>
> Your letter of Dec. 8th just received. I will hasten to answer. Sorry to hear that you have not had such a very good time in Los A. I don't like the place myself. As to conditions of things here—Montgomery has been in. He has turned this property over to Al Davis: that is Al is to handle all bullions and money. There will be no Los Angeles office. Al leaves here in the morning for home and L.A. Al is going to look over the books before taking charge. There has been no leases let. That is all to be settled when Al gets to L.A. I spoke to him this evening about the ground I want. He told me he would get it for [?] if he could. So if I land it if you wish come in the co are going to want the Hulvay [?] lease. I told Al if I got that ground I intended to take you for a partner, that is if you cared to tackle it. They intend now to run the mill all winter, so if I get the ground I would put a man to work or pay my partners half wages or whatever is customary here. Just as soon as Al gets things arranged they are going to put on 8 or 10 men. Henderson has traced the E vein over the hill toward the hoist and has so I am told made quite a strike. And they seem to think they have quite a tonnage of ore in sight. We have had a hell of a time with the pipe line. Took nearly a month to mill Davis & Remby [?] ore. Their ore averaged about $40.00. We are now milling co ore which is of a good grade. I think about $85 stuff. After ____ [remaining pages missing]

Unfortunately, the additional page or pages of the letter have been lost, along with the identity of the writer. Whatever Jim's disappointment in his Los Angeles trip, he had apparently written to his correspondent—and potential partner—from Beatty in early December and received a hopeful report from Skidoo in return.

A different correspondent wrote to Jim from Skidoo on December 28. As with the earlier letter, the handwriting is difficult to read:

> Dear friend Jim
>
> Your letter of 23rd inst. at hand. I have been expecting to hear from you long ago. I am very sorry to say that I took in an other party on the same proposition that you made me. You know Jim that I asked you several times before you left if you stake me should I get the lease. not once you said that you would and on one occasion you said you would not have anything to do with it. With all that I have been expecting to hear from you as I thought that you would stake me should I get the lease. When Montgomery was here about three weeks ago he said we could get the lease if the sale he got on don't go through and he let us know in couple of weeks. All this time I waited for you and only few days ago I had to get someone to stake me. I promised not to reveal ___ [remaining pages missing]

The subsequent pages of the letter are lost along with the writer's signature. But a 1915 letter in the same hand reveals the correspondent's identity as Dick Roschl, an apparent friend and business associate of Jim's. In December 1913, Roschl's regrettable tidings that he has found another partner to stake him in a new lease—however diplomatically communicated—must have come as a tough blow to Jim. Apparently out of work, living on his reserves and casting about for other ventures or stakes, Jim had missed out on a potentially rewarding opportunity with Dick Roschl. And it would appear that Al Davis didn't come through on the promise of a lease to the other unidentified friend. There is no further record or evidence of Jim's residing and working in Skidoo. In 1914, after more than twenty years of prospecting, Jim inexplicably shucked the curse that drove him in search for hidden mineral treasures. He was forty-three years old and may have realized that gold-mining work was for younger men—strong and energetic ones—and that was a model he no longer fit.[14]

My grandfather had come to the end of his gold-mining adventure. For nearly a quarter of a century he had been swallowed up in the western gold rush. In an era when for every ten years a miner worked in the western gold mines chances were one in three he would suffer a serious injury and one in eight he would be killed, Jim Hargrove had survived the perilous mining trade and its sometimes lawless boomtowns.[15] He beat the odds and managed to stay alive and solvent. Best of all, however, he was blessed with an opportunity to pursue an obsession and dream. And although he had not found the fortune that he sought, it seems that he was surely a most fortunate man. By now Jim, of all people, would have realized the necessity of returning home to stake his rightful claim to his inheritance from Captain Hack.

A Fortune Found

Sometime in early 1914, after settling what affairs he could in Skidoo, Beatty, and Townsend, Jim Hargrove returned to the valley of his origins in Haywood County. The following year Dick Roschl wrote to inform Jim that "a party" wanted to buy one of the houses he still owned in Skidoo. If he was smart he didn't waste time in replying and taking advantage of this opportunity—in just a couple more years Skidoo would be no more than a ghost town.

Jim's return home would have fostered joyful reunions with his sister and brothers, and the once intimate siblings would have delighted at the closure of such an extended estrangement. All were married with families: at the time Florence had six children; Joe had six; Theodore had three; and Walter was the proud father of one daughter. Suddenly, after all those long, lonely years, the once solitary prospector had a large family close around him again. Sister, brothers, nieces, nephews, and in-laws were numerous to behold. And it was not long before Jim became acquainted with the widowed sister of Mary Hargrove, his brother Joe's wife. Margaret (Maggie) Shook Evans was twenty-seven and the mother of two young children, Lois and Roy. Apparently he was smitten immediately by Maggie and her kids because in just a few short months, on February 19, 1915, the couple were married in Asheville, North Carolina.

Jim Hargrove and Maggie soon built a house with a barn and assorted outbuildings on the property inherited from Captain Hack. It was a lovely spot nestled between the Pigeon River and steep Pressley Mountain with a vista to the southeast, where Cold Mountain loomed over the Pigeon Valley. In addition to starting up the new farm place the newlyweds quickly got down to the business of raising a family. Their marriage would eventually spawn four beautiful girls—Nannie, Ellen, Mildred, and Jimmie.

It seems to me that my grandfather, Jim Hargrove, was looking in the wrong spot all along for his treasure. After spending many years futilely searching for it out West, he returned home to the Pigeon Valley—there to strike gold when he found Maggie, and to rear the children that were their good fortune.

Jim Hargrove spent many years out West searching for gold, but he had to return to the Pigeon Valley to find his treasure—a wife and family. The four daughters of Jim and Maggie Shook Hargrove, c. 1930, clockwise from upper left: Nannie, Ellen, Mildred, and Jimmie. (Collection of the author.)

The Hargrove siblings, c. early 1940s, clockwise from upper left: Ellen, Jimmie, Nannie, and Mildred. (Collection of the author.)

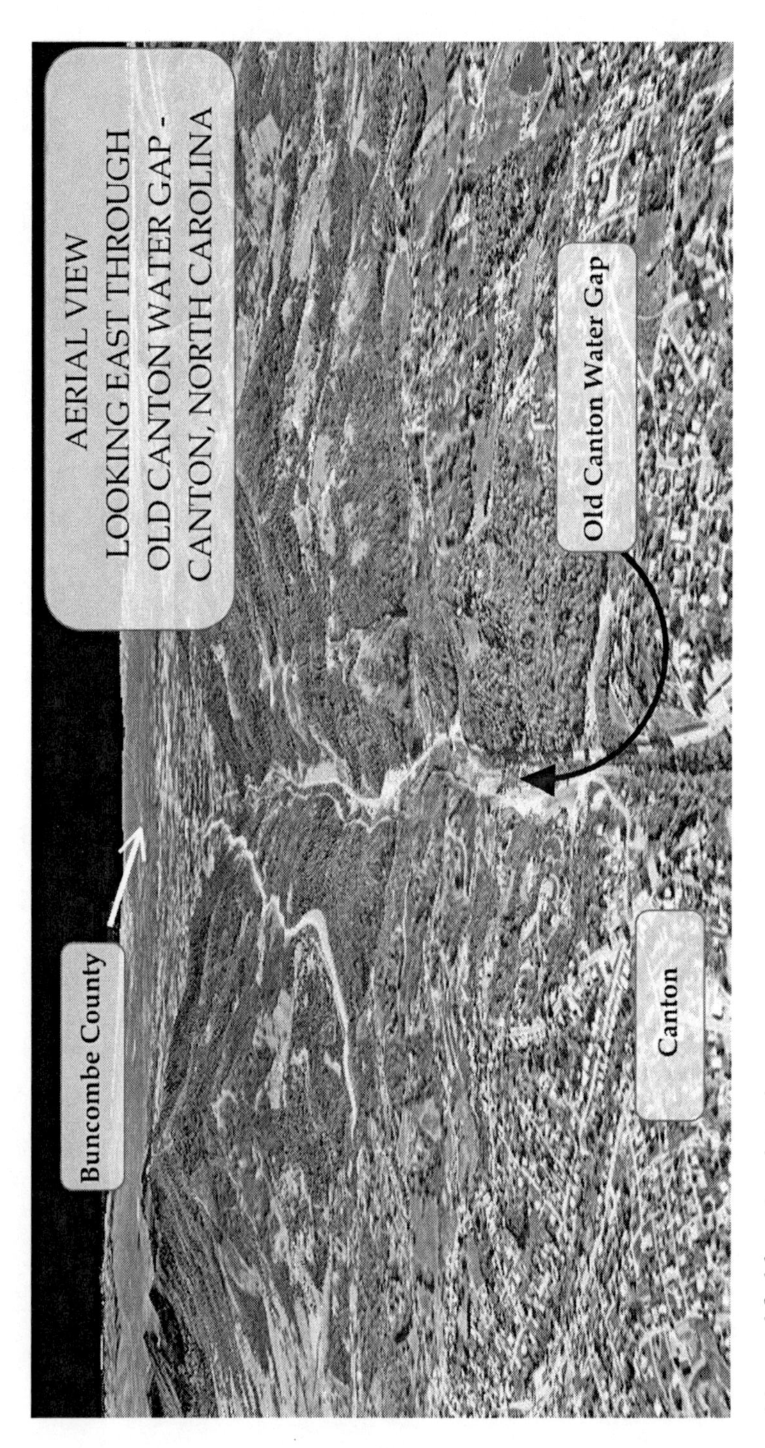

Map modified from GoogleEarth

8 The Old Canton Water Gap

There is a gap in the Newfound Mountain Range, just east of where Canton straddles the Pigeon River today, through which General Griffith Rutherford led a Revolutionary War army to make war with the Cherokee Indians.[1] A century later railroad engineers would find this same gap convenient for their iron rails to penetrate the lofty ramparts and let the tide of civilization and industry flow into the remote mountains of Haywood County. However, millions of years before these relatively recent historical events occurred, this same breach in the Newfounds served another purpose—one for which it would become known to some geologists and chroniclers of history as the "old Canton water gap."

Haywood County historian W. C. Allen recorded in *The Annals of Haywood County, North Carolina* a fanciful notion that eons ago an enormous river drained all of the waters of the Pigeon Valley, Haywood County, and the extreme western region of North Carolina. However, this ancient river did not flow toward the west into the Mississippi River and subsequently the Gulf of Mexico, as the Pigeon

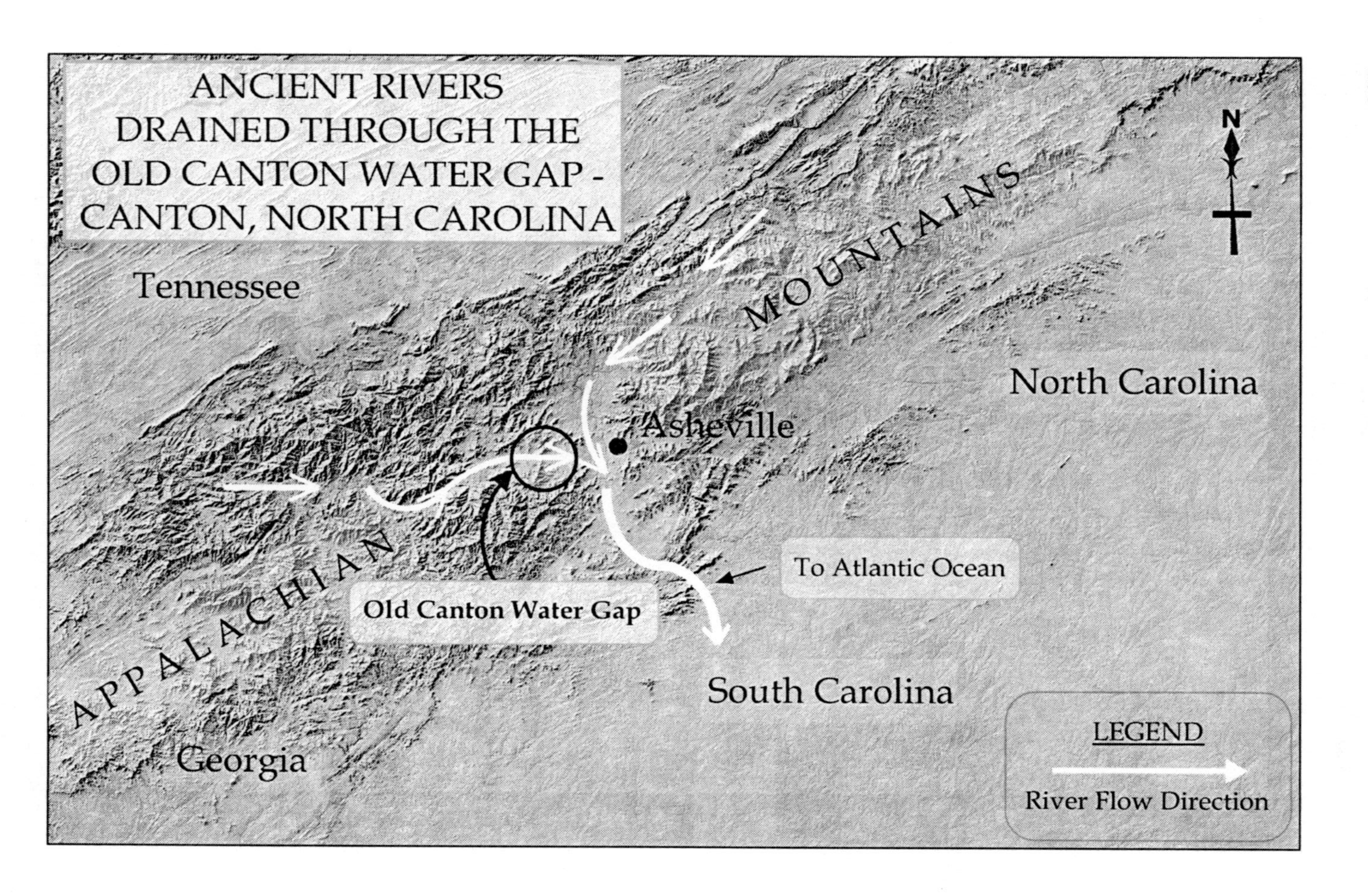
ANCIENT RIVERS
DRAINED THROUGH THE
OLD CANTON WATER GAP -
CANTON, NORTH CAROLINA
N
Tennessee
MOUNTAINS
North Carolina
Asheville
APPALACHIAN
To Atlantic Ocean
Old Canton Water Gap
South Carolina
Georgia
LEGEND
River Flow Direction

River does today. Instead it coursed in an easterly direction through an opening in the mountains near Canton and eventually spilled into the Atlantic Ocean. It seems that this old Canton water gap, as he referred to the mountain breach near Canton—the same one that was so effectively used by General Rutherford and the railroaders to gain entrance into the mountains—served at one time in the distant geological past as a gateway to facilitate a giant river's escape of its mountain confines on a meandering journey to the sea.[2]

To understand the theory that Allen presented, and how the old Canton water gap may have been formed, requires one to consider the tectonic history of the Appalachian Mountain range and the geologic events occurring over hundreds of millions of years that formed them. Yes, *hundreds* of millions—and this measure of time should not be read too quickly or taken lightly for that matter. Few can even comprehend such a breadth of time that is a million years—a relatively short period of geological time, yet five times longer than modern human beings have walked upon this earth.[3] Thus it should be understood that the cataclysmic, geological, and weathering forces of nature that combined to shape the Appalachian Mountains occurred over a period of time almost unfathomable to the human mind.

Publications by the United States Geological Survey and National Park Service indicate that the Appalachian Mountains originated more than 400 million years ago, during the earliest period of the Paleozoic era. In an event that geologists term the Taconic Orogeny, an oceanic plate of the earth's crust began sliding under a passive crust plate to create a zone of subduction at the interface or border of contact. The extreme pressures and heat generated by the forces of two of the planet's plate crusts colliding with each other spawned volcanoes in the so-called zone of subduction where the collision occurred. Volcanic eruptions formed peaks and spewed ash and lava, which blanketed the landscape with layers of igneous rock. In addition, the sedimentary rock deposited in previous ages on the top passive plate began to be uplifted as the oceanic plate continued to push and fold underneath the upper plate. Thus, more mountains were built up and streams began to form which gradually cut the mountains away again with their erosive torrents. Rock, debris, and sediment were carried to lower elevations and deposited to form new layers of sedimentary rock. In this manner, longer ago than we can contemplate and through a process exceedingly difficult to understand, the early Appalachians were born.

Scientists do not know how many land masses or continents existed on earth in those long-ago times. However, they confidently suggest that approximately a dozen plate crusts make up the earth's outer shell, and these have been shifting and moving and crashing into each other since the genesis of the earth and the time when land and water formed upon it. After the Appalachians began to form, the mountain-building plate collisions continued as continent after continent collided and melded together to create a supercontinent called Pangea. It is thought that the Appalachian range had grown to Himalayan proportions by the time Pangea was completely developed, approximately 240 million years ago.

Sometime around 220 million years ago the Pangean supercontinent began to break apart, and the land mass that would eventually become the continent of North America rifted and drifted away from Pangea. As a result, tectonic forces that created the Appalachians were stilled, and a cycle of weathering and erosion prevailed that began to wear away the mountains. By the end of the Mesozoic Era some 65 million years ago—about the time of the great dinosaur extinction—the Appalachian Mountain terrain had been worn down to an almost flat plain, perhaps only a few hundred feet above sea level. Thence and throughout the current Cenozoic Era until the present day, uplifting caused by ongoing plate collisions has rejuvenated streams, and familiar weathering and erosion forces have been constantly at work to produce the distinctive topography recognized today as the Appalachian Mountains.

In the present day the Appalachians cover a huge, almost unbroken expanse over 1,500 miles long and often a couple hundred miles wide. They extend from Alabama and Georgia at the southern extremity to Canada at the northern tip. The current Southern highlands topography, in which western North Carolina lies, is largely the work of never-resting rivers and, to a lesser extent, nature's weathering forces of wind, rain, heat, and cold. Uplifted plains have been gradually eaten away over millions and millions of years by the relentless hydraulic forces of the streams. Under an unremitting influence of the laws of physics and gravity, these small creeks and large rivers cut away at the softer rock to forge deep ravines and valleys. The harder rock is left in place to form recognizable features such as the high peaks, crags, pinnacles, and domes as the rushing waters of the rivers forge their paths to the sea.[4]

W. C. Allen writes that at the end of the Mesozoic Age 65 million years ago, western North Carolina was a broad, flat plain with sluggish rivers meandering throughout. It was marked then, as it is today, by two areas of higher elevation—the Great Smoky Mountains to the west and the Blue Ridge Range in the east. These mountain ranges ran parallel with one another in a northeast-to-southwest direction and were probably comprised of only low, rounded hills reaching elevations no higher than 3,000 feet above sea level. During that age, as now, the Great Smokies were slightly higher in elevation and formed the divide of streams flowing to the western Gulf waters and those seeking the Atlantic Ocean.

The expansive and relatively flat valley between these two mountain ranges was drained by two main rivers. One had its source in the northern Appalachian highlands of today's North Carolina and western Virginia territories and ran along a southwesterly course to the vicinity where Asheville is currently located. The other river originated in North Carolina's western extremity and flowed in a northeastward direction, eventually passing through the water gap at Canton and then joining up with the previously mentioned stream just beyond in the Asheville vicinity.

This second river, which fell out of the Great Smokies in the far west, gathered up enormous volumes of water on its route out of the mountains. Topographic features visible today and geologic evidence reveal that its ancient course passed through the modern areas of Topton, Bryson City, Sylva, and Balsam Gap. From there it flowed through the Haywood County regions of Waynesville, Lake Junaluska, and Clyde, and then, after collecting the Pigeon Valley drainage, made its escape through the old Canton water gap. The monster river continued along a bed still utilized today by Hominy Creek to join up in the French Broad Valley with the other principal river draining from the north. The combined waters of these two prehistoric watercourses escaped the Blue Ridge and meandered through the South Carolina coastal region to the Atlantic Ocean, whose waves washed ashore several hundred miles inland from where they do today.

For millions of years the waters of the region presently delineated as Haywood County were gathered up by this ancient lazy river and carried over a now extinct riverbed through the gap in today's Newfound Mountains—the old Canton water gap. And only after more gradual uplifting of the region occurred and the resulting swifter mountain streams devoured significant portions of the softer rock of the Great Smokies did the drainage patterns begin to change.

Near the region of Hartford, Tennessee, at a point now known as Waterville, a ruthless mountain stream, or streams, finally succeeded in cutting a small breach through the Great Smoky Mountains. This opening presented a more favorable gradient for the waters on the eastern side of the divide to flow westward toward the Gulf of Mexico. Over a very long period of time the waters of the ancient monster river were gradually tapped to drain through this new path of less resistance and through other similar paths that would form new rivers such as the Hiwassee and Little Tennessee rivers. The once bold water body slowly dwindled in size until it eventually reversed course entirely, and today's Pigeon River was born to drain Haywood County's waters to the Gulf of Mexico.

Coincidental with the birth of the Pigeon River was the demise of the old Canton water gap. However, little Hominy Creek still lives and defiantly flows today just east of Canton. Forever patient, it faithfully keeps to the ancient extinct river's bed as it races toward Asheville and the French Broad River. Fascinating as it may seem, W. C. Allen noted in his history of Haywood County that this small, seemingly passive stream is gradually, little by little, eroding and cutting its way backward toward the Pigeon River—with the inevitable result that one day, maybe centuries or a millennium or a million years in the future, the Pigeon River will be diverted from its present course to once again flow eastward through the old Canton water gap.

Opposite: Maggie Hargrove in the yard of her Pigeon Valley farmhouse, c. 1960s. (Collection of the author.)

9 Granny Hargrove's House

"I'M GOING TO THE COUNTRY. WHO'S COMING?" Mother would yell, knowing very well the immediate response from her two sons. These were magical words to my brother and me back when we were growing up in Canton in the 1950s and '60s. A trip to the country was a highly anticipated event, and we anxiously awaited any opportunity to visit the farm where our mother was born and raised. That would be the same place where Granny Hargrove lived—right smack in the middle of the rural farming community of Pigeon Valley, in Haywood County.

The Old River Road

Most every weekend we were accustomed to visiting our Granny Hargrove and Aunt Nannie and Uncle Tommy, who lived in the old homeplace. Nannie, my mother's sister, was married to Tommy Smathers. Together they had kept the farm going after my grandfather's death in 1937. Grandfather James Burton Hargrove was a descendant of William Manson Hartgrove and Joseph Cathey, both pioneer settlers of the Pigeon Valley in the early 1800s. After years of prospecting for gold out West, my grandfather found his way back to the Pigeon Valley and promptly married the recently widowed Margaret Hazeltine Shook Evans, who eventually became known to a younger generation of the family as Granny Hargrove. Together they established the farm and set about spawning and rearing a large family of five girls and one boy.

Granny Hargrove, or Maggie, as friends called her, was descended from Jacob Shook, who was among the earliest pioneers to enter Haywood County at the end of the eighteenth century and settle along the Pigeon River. In the frame house he proudly built near Clyde he hosted the traveling Methodist minister, Bishop Francis Asbury, during the esteemed clergyman's journeys through the area. One can easily see how rich was my heritage and how I might have grown to love a little mountain farmstead in the Pigeon Valley and way out in the country.

Granny Hargrove's farm was only four or five miles south of Canton up the Pigeon River and located in the heart of the Pigeon Valley. It was situated just opposite where an iron bridge had been erected to span the river and link the Old River Road, which ran along the "back side" of the river, to the paved road, now known as Highway 110. After my brother and I sorted out seating options and determined who would have the privilege of riding shotgun, we would head up the back side of the river in our new green Dodge. This newfangled automobile possessed the latest technological

The Hargrove-Smathers farmstead, looking toward the bottom fields and the Pigeon River in the distance, c. 1950s. The iron truss bridge still spans the stream and the Old River Road still courses along its bank. (Collection of the author.)

advances—push-button transmission and high, shiny fins mimicking the latest jet airplane designs at the time, and we were proud of it. My father normally didn't accompany us on these jaunts, so it was usually just the three of us—Mother, my brother, Rego, and me. Sometimes Aunt Ellen, who lived across the street from us, would make it a foursome. Penland Street, a two-lane paved avenue, led southward past the football stadium and schools and finally the recreation park to the outskirts of Canton, where it made two quick crossings of the Pigeon River over dated wooden-timbered bridges. Just past the second bridge we encountered the Old River Road, where the street abruptly transitioned to an unimproved gravel and sand road that hugged the riverbank closely all the way to Granny's.

The route along the Old River Road toward Bethel passed familiar points of interest. A cutoff led to Granny Hargrove's Piney Grove Methodist Church, harbored deep within Stamey Cove's mountain walls. In later years this secluded cove would host the little nine-hole Mountain View Golf Course where my brother and I would discover the joy and frustrations of that most difficult game. Taking notice from the passenger-side windows as we passed the road leading into the Stamey Cove, we continued along the Old River Road and soon were abreast of Claude Rhinehart's house.

Approaching Claude's we would almost always ask Mom to slow down. We strained to get a good view out of the passenger-side windows, and our hopes rose as we tried to spy the simple farmer on the front porch of his little frame house or maybe get a look at his mule grazing out in the pasture. Claude was always dressed in overalls and never appeared without an oversized wad of tobacco in his mouth. In the springtime he could be seen throughout the Valley and Canton breaking ground and plowing behind his old mule. Almost directly across from Claude's place, at a severe bend in the Pigeon River, a deep pool had formed over the centuries. Mom warned us many a time of the dangers of that place and explained how there was a whirlpool there that would suck a person under to drown if ever caught in its deadly clutch. I never forgot her advice, either, and was always a little anxious when rafting past that perilous spot on old inner tubes during the sultry summers.

On up the river road a ways we could peek through the trees to the right and get a good glimpse of Daddy Paw's house perched over on the hillside. Daddy Paw was Joe Hargrove, my grandfather's brother, who was a famed bear hunter in the mountains. It was not unusual following hunting season to see a bear hide or two stretched out and nailed to the side of his barn, fur side in, to dry and cure. And somewhere along that same bottom stretch was an old fording place where for more than a century farmers and pioneers crossed the river on horseback and in horse-drawn wagons. It was so shallow at times that the local folk could drive their cars right off into the middle of the river to wash them—at least that's what Mom told us. Seemed to me to be a peculiar notion; it would be just as easy to use a water hose and bucket of soapy water, but then again I was just a young'un and what did I know, anyhow? I never did see anybody washing their cars in the river.

Farther up the way was a pretty stretch of fertile bottomland, mostly owned by the Hargroves. I remember seeing men at work making molasses near the edge of one of those fields right in there. A horse harnessed to a sugar cane press was walking around in circles to drive the machine and squeeze out the juices from the freshly cut cane. In the fall right before the first frost hit was molasses-making time, when the cane stalks were ripest and heavily laden with their rich liquid. An old brick kiln stood for years at that spot (until the state built the new road through the bottom), and that was where they boiled down the yellowish-green cane juice to render the golden-colored molasses. I remember seeing smoke billowing away from the busy affair and wondering just what in the world they had on fire in there.

For years molasses was an important food staple for the farmers in the Valley. It had many culinary applications and was used as a substitute for sugar when times got hard and sugar got scarce or too expensive to buy. Granny always had a jar of molasses on her kitchen table. I can remember trying it with cornbread. I can't say that I liked it much, but I did like hot biscuits smeared generously with molasses and butter. Granny used to say that it would stick to your bones all day.

Just past Uncle Joe's about a half mile or so was the old iron truss bridge. For many years that useful structure provided the primary means for the local farmers and motorists to cross the river and gain access to either side of the Pigeon Valley. The one-lane bridge, a simple design consisting of two fabricated steel trusses spanning the river over concrete abutments on each side, had been built sometime in the early years of the twentieth century. The timbered road flooring was supported from the bottom of the trusses, while stiffening members joined the two trusses together at the top. From afar it shone bright and silvery, like a steel tower or cage fallen over on its side. Mother recounted often how she and her sisters used to climb all over that bridge like monkeys. She said that Granny would scream until she was hoarse, from way over at the house several hundred yards away, for them to get down off that bridge. Poor Granny must have suffered a sight at times raising those mischievous girls of hers.

Nannie Hargrove Smathers in the front yard of Granny Hargrove's farmhouse surrounded by a passel of Jim and Maggie Hargrove's grandsons, c. 1955. Left to right: Jim Holbrook, Rego Jones, Tommy Holbrook (with bandage on forehead), Carroll Jones, Bill Holbrook (taking dead aim at the photographer), and Doby Holbrook. (Collection of the author.)

Granny's House

From this strategic crossroads one could either veer to the left over the bridge and cross the river, or keep on heading straight ahead as the Old River Road coursed in behind where Bill Holbrook lives today and passed the Moore property toward Woodrow and Bethel. The other option was the one that we favored and always took, and that was to bear to the right onto a dirt lane leading off through the cornfields and across the old railroad bed to Granny's. From the bridge we could see her house easily, unless the corn was in season and had grown so big that it blocked our view. To my eyes it was as picturesque a setting as you ever wanted to see—a little white farmhouse nestled at the foot of Pressley Mountain about a quarter mile away. It wasn't fancy, mind you, just simple, plain, and pretty to look at.

I always wondered how my grandfather settled on that exact spot and orientation to build his home. Surely he wanted a site that would be high and dry and above the potential flooding ravages of the Pigeon River, so he chose well in that respect. And he must have desired to take full advantage of his property's ideal southeastern exposure on the mountain slope to capture as much heat from the winter sun as possible. The old Champion railroad to Sunburst ran right through his property at that time, and he needed to stay a good ways back from the right-of-way lest the noise and smoke and fire hazard from the trains present a nuisance. And whether or not he considered the vista of Cold Mountain looming off in the distance toward the south is a matter of conjecture. In the day when he constructed his house—around 1920—the mountain had not gained the notoriety that it enjoys today. The scene of a World War II–era bomber crash in 1946 and the setting for a best-selling novel of that name by Charles Frazier, Cold Mountain is indeed the dominating geographical feature of the area, after the river. I don't believe my grandfather was mindful of that, though, as he contemplated where to build a house for Granny Hargrove.

That narrow trace through the cornfield bottom leading over to Granny's offered a variety of scenes as we passed through in our car, depending on the time of year. In the summer the corn would grow so high and dense on both sides of the little pathway that the sun would disappear, it seemed, as we drove through. Late fall and winter presented a lonely expanse of grayish brown soil dotted everywhere with cornstalk stubbles and littered with shreds of fodder. Cornstalks and fodder were leaned up in shocks around the field, resembling teepees and giving the impression of an old Indian village beside the lazy river. As winter gradually gave way to the arrival of spring we watched for Uncle Tommy turning and plowing and dressing the fields in preparation for the next corn and tobacco crops.

When I saw that those fields had been plowed my heart would start beating a little faster. Hopes would swell that Mom or Aunt Nannie might take me out there to look for some treasures like those hidden away in the shoe box in Granny's closet. Not gold or diamonds, no, but like the things mysteriously left behind by the Indians that were scattered all across Granny's field. That old worn shoe box of hers was filled with beautiful artifacts that the Hargrove girls had found over the years such as pieces of broken pottery, some with designs or even fingerprints of the ancient potter impressed in the clay. In the box were an ax head and several arrowheads, bird points, spear points, scrapers, and small stone discs that Nannie said were Indian game pieces. The sight of that plowed field always stirred romantic thoughts of ancient relics in my mind. And it provoked powerful and hopeful feelings of walking along side of Nannie and Mother, scooping up Indian treasures made and used and left behind so long ago.

We never knew just what was in store for us as we drove down that rutted dirt road through the bottom fields, but we knew with the confident certainty of youth that our Granny would be expecting us, and we could not wait to lay eyes on her. Often Granny would be out in the yard piddling in her flower garden as we drove up and parked underneath a giant weeping willow at the foot of the steep bank fronting her house. If the sun was high in the sky, she would likely be wearing one of the huge colorful bonnets that she herself had fashioned to protect her face from the sun. The bonnet covered her entire head, ears and neck, and had a short little visor and tie strings that fastened under her chin to secure it snuggly in place. My brother and I would race up the bank over a flight of rough rock steps leading to the house and see who could beat the other to hug Granny first.

How we loved her! I can remember thinking how pretty she was. She didn't seem old at all to us. We liked to tease her and ask if she was dipping some snuff. Granny really liked her snuff—but I remember once, when she took some out of her mouth and smeared it over a nasty bee sting I had gotten, how it almost made me sick at my stomach.

"Shoooooo, Granny, what you doing?" I whined.

"Don't you worry none," she replied. "That'll make the pain better, so hold this kerchief over it and leave it there a spell." Granny did not talk a lot, and I loved to be around her and watch her stringing and breaking beans and knitting and cooking cornbread and canning and all those "country" kinds of things. Although she was probably not conscious of doing so, Granny was demonstrating to her grandson his heritage, and she must have done it well because he would never forget those lessons.

The house my grandfather constructed for Granny was just a simple frame structure built on a sloping hillside. The cinder-block foundation was head-high at the front of the house and dug into the hill on the backside, an arrangement that offered some basement space that was put to good use in the early days before electricity and a modern refrigerator arrived. Under the house they built a concrete trough to hold water sluiced from the well that was located just outside the basement wall. There, in the cool bath of water, was where the milk, butter, cream and clabber were stored in warm weather to keep it from spoiling. Granny also kept in that dugout basement all of her canning products, preserves, taters, apples and such that would feed her family during the cold mountain winters.

A screened porch ran across the entire front elevation of the house and wrapped around the left side, extending about halfway to the rear. Cement steps led up to the main door in front, while a flight of wooden steps gained entry to the side porch adjacent to the kitchen. The house was clad in horizontal wood lapped siding that was whitewashed, and it was covered by a rusty, red-colored metal roof. Mother always said that she loved going to sleep with the sound of the raindrops pitter-pattering steadily on the thin metal over her head. There must have been occasions, too, when the noise overhead was thunderous and threatening and may even have scared her as a young child. As a farmer's daughter, though, she would have appreciated at an early age the life-giving qualities of a good rainfall and its relationship to the prosperity of her family's little enterprise there on the banks of the Pigeon River.

Mother used to tell us lots of tales about growing up in the country. We could sit for hours listening to them and worrying her with our questions—sometimes just plain foolish ones but most of the time innocent and honest inquiries. She didn't mind talking about her life growing up, either. Even though her family lived simply and had a hard time of it during those rough Depression years, it was obvious that she had a wonderful childhood with two loving and caring parents. And of course there were a host of sisters who were thick as thieves.

"What did you do in the wintertime when you had to go to the bathroom, Mommy?" That surely was one of those crazy questions that either Rego or I asked, and we would just lie there in the floor, wide-eyed and staring up at our mother, listening for what she was going to answer and thinking ahead to what we might ask next. It is still hard for me to believe that she grew up in a house in the country without electricity or running water or inside bathroom. Like two little machine guns we rattled off questions at her, and she would patiently try to answer the best she could. "Was it hard for a girl to use a pee pot?" or "Where did you get all those Sears catalogs, Mom?" and "Did you go to the outhouse at night? How did you see?" or "Was it hard to do your homework using a kerosene lamp?" Those are the types of things we would ask and want to know, and there were thousands more just like them. And with her responses and explanations we learned from her as much as any schoolteacher or professor ever taught us. And we became more aware of who we were and grew to appreciate what we had and what our mother and father sacrificed for us.

Just as you topped those steps at the screened back porch—right inside the screening—was where Granny used to hang her leather-britches and peppers to dry. There the hot afternoon sun bore in and would do the best job of drying. I was always curious about those leather-britches, and it was a long time before I learned they were just cornfield beans dried out in the sun to keep until needed for nourishment during the long winters. The back door leading into the kitchen was on the left just past that spot where the leather-britches were hung. We spent most of our time in the kitchen, it seems now as I think back. My brother and I would sit and watch and listen mostly as Granny, Nannie, and Mom and her sisters went about their cooking or canning chores or just huddled to talk.

As the womenfolk visited and worked, my gaze would eventually start to wander around the room, taking in all the familiar sights. Hanging on a peg just inside the door were my Uncle Tommy's old caps and work coat that he wore. His coat always smelled like fuel oil, having soaked up splatters and odors over the years. He and Nannie owned and operated Smathers' Fuel Oil Company in Canton, and he worked endless hours delivering heating oil to customers night and day and in all weather conditions. The caps were emblazoned with the logos of Ford or John Deere or Esso, and occasionally I would take one down and wear it around, proud to look like Uncle Tommy and just like a farmer.

Close to where the caps hung, a coffee grinder was mounted on the wall. I don't remember ever seeing it used, but Mom recalled for me that she was accustomed to awaking in the mornings as a young girl to the sound and smell of her parents grinding coffee beans in that little mill. Next to the coffee grinder was the old Hoosier cabinet where Nannie and Granny kept some of their foodstuffs and glass and flatware. That was, also, the place where they kept the flour in the bin over the sifter and the sugar in another special compartment in the bottom. Next to the old Hoosier sat an antique oak sideboard where dishes and china and other miscellaneous things were stored. Hidden away deep inside this piece of furniture was the jar of gold dust that our grandfather had unearthed out West when he was a young man. Anytime Granny or Nannie removed that precious jar from its hiding place for us presented another opportunity for them to recount for us the stories of our grandfather's Wild West adventures and how he came to discover that gold.

Along the opposite wall of the kitchen was where we could sit around the kitchen table and look out a window at the rising mountain backdropping the house—always trying to catch a glimpse of a fox or hawk or turkey or even one of Uncle Tommy's cows. Above the sink was a smaller window that offered a view of an expansive yard and the barn and outbuildings, and in the distance beyond, the stately old Moore house. From this vantage point Granny for years had kept an eye out for her girls. She watched to make sure they weren't sneaking around behind the barn smoking rabbit tobacco, or she admired how her girls' skills were improving at shooting a basketball through an old iron barrel hoop nailed to the side of the barn. And from that same window Nannie stayed on the lookout for Tommy coming out of the fields or arriving home from work, and for her daughter, Nancy, playing in the yard or around the barn.

Nancy was our first cousin. An only child, she was several years older than Rego and me, so we didn't have real opportunities to actually play with her. We used to watch her ride her horse, Sassabo, in shows and look on from the roadside as she strutted by in parades twirling a baton and leading the high school band as a majorette. Mom would even ride us up to the country now and then to get a look at Nancy all dressed up and ready to go to a prom or some other fancy affair—just as pretty as she could be. It was really something when she went off to college at Chapel Hill, and we were all excited and just proud to be her relation.

During the summer, after all the work was done in the kitchen or after we had eaten and all the dishes were cleaned and put away, everyone would mosey out to the big screened porch at the front of the house. From there we could sit and rock and take advantage of the fresh evening breezes and look out over the cornfield and the river toward the beautiful Blue Ridge Mountains to the south and east. Nannie would point out for us the old tree leaning over the river and allow how Mildred and Jimmie were the only girls in the area brave enough to climb way up to the top of that tree and dive off into the pond below, the "Martha Jaybird" swimming hole, as they called it.

I will never forget that old porch. It had a floor made of narrow pine boards so old that some of them had holes left where the knots had dried and fallen out. One night, I can remember, just about dusky dark as we were admiring the lighting bugs and their pyrotechnics show, I heard a faint scratching noise down around my feet. For the life of me I was not able to make out what in the world it was. Expecting it to be some sort of insect suffering its last throes of existence, I hunched over real low from the rocking chair to get a better look in the dim light. Well, about that time, "bigger than Pete," something popped up out of one of those knot holes at me just like a snake. I am not usually one prone to dramatics, but that time I jumped back and screamed so loud that I guess they could hear me way over on the other side of the river.

Everybody began laughing and pointing, and when I spotted Mom rounding the corner and walking toward me with a big grin from ear to ear I knew she had played a trick to scare me. She picked me up and hugged me and said, "Everything's going to be all right, baby." Come to find out that while we were all gabbing away and distracted she had sneaked off down into the basement under the porch floor. Right below where I was sitting she had made that little scratching sound to get my attention and then jabbed her finger through the knothole and wiggled it away. Well, no harm done, right? I don't know so much about that because after more than half a century that memory is as vivid as if it had been seared into my brain only yesterday. I have never been so scared in all my born days.

The Farm

Several outbuildings surrounded the house back then, including the barn next to which grew a good-sized cherry tree. Its delicious crimson fruit was offered each year to those daring enough to climb it, or to the birds—whoever got there first. The smokehouse sat just on the hill above the barn, and somewhere in that vicinity an old outhouse stood lonely and abandoned but seemingly still vigilant and ready for another late-night visit from one of those young Hargrove girls. The barn was rustic and crudely built, with siding made of rough sawn lumber that was stained black, and a rusting metal gambrel roof. Just inside the sliding barn door nearest the house was a large open space where Tommy stored everything from tractor attachments like plows, tillers, and disc harrows to old tools, gasoline and lubrication products, milk cans, and horse tack—saddles, bridles, harnesses, and such. I remember there were also some other old relics hanging on the walls—singletrees, doubletrees, and old horse collars—which undoubtedly were implements that had been used in Granddaddy Hargrove's day.

It was so dark when you first walked into the barn that you could just barely see, until your eyes eventually adjusted to the low light conditions. That moment was the spookiest. We knew that there were snakes in there, and nobody cared, because they helped control the mice. And there were a bunch of wild cats and kittens that hung around in the barn, and nobody cared about that either, because they too controlled the mouse population and kept the snakes down to a tolerable level. So given those circumstances we tended to be a little nervous and timorous when entering the barn and until we could see around the floor and into the dark corners.

Mother was always strict about not letting us go into the stable area because she was afraid that we could get stepped on or kicked by the livestock. But when Aunt Nannie was milking we would stand right behind her, big-eyed and open-mouthed, and watch as she squeezed the cow's teats up and down and squirted the milk into a tin pail. And if one of those wild cats came sniffing around and got within range she sometimes would take deadly aim and shoot a stream of milk in its direction just so to tickle us. I tried my best to learn how to milk but I never could get the hang of it, no matter which way I squeezed those things.

The barn loft where Uncle Tommy kept the hay stored was accessed by a wooden ramp leading up from the hillside where it had been dug out for the barn. It was mostly off limits to us because the floor had holes in it for feeding the cattle and horses below. The loft was dark and it was hard to see those holes, which sometimes got covered over with hay, so Mom and Nannie would not let us go up there unless they accompanied us. Besides hay there were a couple of ancient steamer trunks stored there, full of old documents and family papers and other things left over from Granddaddy Hargrove's time. While warning us to watch for the mice, Mother or Nannie would open the trunks and let us rummage through all the mildewed papers and musty-smelling junk inside, until we got tired of it. Back then I had no idea what that stuff was or the value that it might offer to a grandson bent on learning more about his grandfather. Often now, I wish that I could go back in time and sift through those wonderful things one by one and see what might be revealed. My grandfather died thirteen years before I was born, and I never had the privilege of knowing him.

On the hillside above the barn, on that same side where you could walk up the ramp into the loft, stood the old smokehouse. Many years before my time, after hog killings the meat would be butchered and thoroughly salted down and hung up in the smokehouse to cure. The structure, built on poles sunk into the hillside and framed and clad with rough lumber, was about ten feet wide by sixteen feet long. In the cellar underneath, fires were built for smoke to fill the house and cure the meat.

My grandfather would sometimes use the space under the smokehouse to pack away his tobacco after it was hung and cured in the barn, to keep it from drying out too much and "fracturing." The smokehouse was long out of use when we children visited, but we could still peek inside from time to time just to see what might be in there. Plunder—that's about all we ever saw, just a bunch of plunder. The other outbuilding on the farm was the chicken coop located on the opposite side of the house, away from the barn, toward Uncle Joe's. Abandoned and in a dismal state of repair, as I remember, it was just about to fall to pieces. We explored through it often, studying the roost poles and the boxes and trying to figure out how the chickens lived in there and laid their eggs.

Beyond the coop was a big old black walnut tree. Many times we went out there to gather walnuts off the ground and eat them right there on the spot. Sometimes I would go alone, but often times groups of family members would congregate under the tree to break and eat walnuts and talk. After peeling off the outer husk by hand all you had to do was smash the nut between two rocks, open it, and pick out the fruit. A good flat mountain rock was used like an anvil, with a smaller and rounder rock as a hammer. You had to be careful, though, not to smash the nuts too hard, else you would crush the fruit into tiny pieces and crumbs that weren't easily eaten. Those walnuts sure were good to eat. But the best part about those excursions was sitting under the tree on the cool green grass and visiting with all our relations—and the worst part was that our hands would get all stained and black from the juices in the husks and it was hard as the dickens to wash off.

The Mountain

The farm sat right at the foot of Pressley Mountain, which rose very steeply behind the house for more than a thousand feet to an elevation of approximately 3,560 feet above sea level. The lower half of the mountain, which was used to pasture the cattle and horses, was partially wooded with oaks, hickories, walnut, maple, dogwood, locust and poplar trees. The top part, as I recollect, was covered mostly in pines and absent of hardwoods, perhaps as a result of a fire once started up there by the fox hunters. I remember that fire vaguely, even though I was very young, because of how anxious and nervous we all were when Dad climbed up to the top with the other men to fight it. It was hours before they got the fire under control and came back down off the mountain, all tired and covered with soot and dirt.

Although the mountain was plenty steep and a hard climb for us young'uns, we relished the opportunity to tackle it. Behind the house Uncle Tommy had built a clever little gate in the fence that was easy for humans to turn sidewise and walk through, but the cattle and horses were not able to escape through it. After passing this gate we could follow one of the many cow trails around the contour of the mountain slope out toward the walnut tree, taking great care to dodge all the fresh cow piles splattered about. Out near the walnut tree we would turn and head up a little valley passing the Rabbit Rock, a large boulder sticking out of the mountain side that also marked the property line, and going on up to a spring where the cattle watered. Normally we would pause there to get our breath, and maybe even sample the spring water if it was running clear and the cows had not disturbed it too badly.

While resting there for a few minutes we would have a chance to look across the sides of the mountain and down the steep valley we had just climbed. I was always curious about the randomly placed short rock walls laid up at intervals across the hillside. Mother explained that our grandfather had built them by just picking up the weathered mountain rocks which were strewn everywhere and toting and piling them up one on top of the other. She didn't explain why he went to this trouble, probably thinking we were simply too young to comprehend his motives. I can just see our grandfather walking back and forth around that mountainside, hunched over and carrying and stacking rocks to make his low walls. He was a shrewd mountaineer who had been a hard-rock gold miner as a younger man. Those little rock walls of his would help protect the mountain slopes from erosion and washing during heavy mountain cloudbursts and winter rains. Moreover, he was able to clear his pasture of obstacles to win a little more grass-growing ground and to make it easier for the livestock to graze with less risk of stumbling and injury.

Beyond that spring was some hard going. Up high the pasture and hardwoods petered out, and pine woods and dense undergrowth predominated. Undesirable thistle plants grew prolifically for a while, until Uncle Tommy hired a helicopter to spray herbicides to eradicate and control them. Just below the top of the mountain there was an old road that he used occasionally in his Jeep truck to check on the cattle and fences, and a short distance beyond that was the peak of the mountain. There used to be a fox hunters' shack up there high on the mountain, where we relished the opportunity to snoop around and look at their old potbellied stove and whatever else may have been left lying around.

Reaching the top was an exhilarating yet anticlimactic feeling. We felt like conquerors after beating that big old mountain, but because we could not see for the pine trees blocking the sight lines there were no breathtaking panoramic vistas or fabulous sights to behold. We would not tarry very long on the mountaintop—just catch our breath and plot the route back down.

For us young'uns, the trip down was a piece of cake. With the helpful assistance of gravity we could slide down on our backsides most of the way if we had a mind to. It was on one of those quick descents, down near the bottom of the mountain, when we once ran up on a black snake. We were not accustomed to seeing them and this one was spotted from a fair distance, so we were not frightened. I was so confident of our advantage that I picked up a small rock, one my grandfather apparently overlooked in building his walls, and threw it at the snake, thinking all along that I would scare the thing off. As it turned out that snake was not a black snake at all. It was a black *racer* snake, and I had provoked it bigger than Pete. The snake came racing toward us as fast as lighting—and we took off running away from it even faster, hollering and screaming and sprinting the rest of the way down the mountain. We never looked back until we had slammed the back porch door behind us, thankful to be safe and sound inside the house. From that day on I have held black racer snakes in very high regard.

Many more happy memories come to mind as I think back to my childhood experiences at Granny Hargrove's farm. In late August and September the grape arbor vines were always heavily loaded with ripened fruit, and many delightful hours were spent picking the grapes, dodging bees and gorging ourselves with those delicious purple orbs. Seems, too, that I remember a few grape-throwing fights that landed us in a heap of trouble. Just down from the arbor at the foot of the embankment where Mom parked the car was a big weeping willow tree that lent its branches just right for us boys to swing on. We could grab a handful of those hanging limbs, get a good run off the steep bank, and swing ourselves all the way down to the bottom of the hill, just like Tarzan. Man, that was a lot of fun.

I harbor many fond recollections, even though I probably whined and complained at the time, of going into the garden with Granny in the early morning hours while the dew was still beaded on the plants to pick beans, tomatoes, and corn. After that we would sit around in a circle—me and my brother and the womenfolk—with a newspaper spread over our laps and just chat away while shucking the corn or stringing and breaking the beans and tossing them into a big pot. It always seemed such a daunting task when we started, knowing that there was probably a bushel or more of beans to string. But with everyone working, and including my piddling contributions, we could finish off those beans in no time.

Canning was an activity that Mom and her sisters and Granny used to do cooperatively. I am not going to let on here and try to explain their whole process because I don't rightly know it, even though I used to watch them all the time. To this day I associate the kitchen smell of beans, corn, tomatoes, and apples cooking with their canning operation. The contents of these precious jars sustained us Hargroves through the winters, and I still prefer canned green beans cooked with a piece of pork fatback over any other vegetable. Granny also made a special relish concoction from tomatoes and peppers that when heaped over mashed potatoes seemed to make the potatoes go down easier and without too much suffering.

At last when it was time to head back down the river Mother

would holler out "time to go," her words falling on us with the suddenness and force of a clap of thunder. Reluctantly we would say our good-byes and, after giving Granny a big bear hug, run to the willow tree and swing down to the bottom of the hill one last time before piling back into the car. The return trip home was not nearly so interesting; the scenery went unnoticed with the certain, glum realization that a bath was surely in store for us. Not even that dreadful contemplation, though, could dampen the enthusiasm and joy that lingered in our minds and hearts after a visit to Granny Hargrove's house in the Pigeon Valley.

Opposite: Mules draw a sled and power the sorghum mill at this rustic molasses-making manufactory. (Farm Security Administration/Office of War Information Collection, Library of Congress.)

10 Summer: A Time for Growing

Sweltering summer sun and quenching afternoon thunder bursts were the life force and key to survival for the early settlers of the lands along the upper Pigeon River and its tributaries. Longer days and more light, higher temperatures, ample moisture, and fertile soil combined to trigger an eruption of bountiful crops of corn and wheat from the valley bottomlands and hillsides, and tasty fruit and berries from the orchard trees and meadow bushes. The farmers and their families toiled for long hours under the scorching sun to cultivate and harvest these important foodstuffs, but they were accustomed to such. It was the key to their existence. The hardy men, women, and children would have borne their agrarian burdens comfortably, satisfied that only by their extreme exertions would they have food aplenty to get them through the next harsh mountain winter.

Rows and rows of young corn and tobacco plants required constant attention, and the Valley's farmers, wielding hoes and sticks, constantly battled the weeds until the crops needed no more defending. "Laid by," it was called, when no more hoeing was necessary and the young men and girls could then breathe a sigh of relief.[1] Their attentions were subsequently directed to the mountain meadows, where raspberry, blackberry, and huckleberries were ripe and awaited picking. And it was not uncommon for groups of young folk to gather on berry-picking excursions, when collecting the wild fruit and courting sometimes mingled and many a romance began. Everybody knew that if a girl "weren't no good" at berrying then she would not rightly be good at marrying.

The early weeks of summer found the men folk usually engaged with harvesting the winter grain crops—wheat, barley, rye, and oats. From dawn until dusk they labored with their sharpened scythes and cradles, mowing the grain grasses; whole families would be enlisted to follow behind, grasping and binding bundles of grain together and shocking them in piles. Later the shocks would be hauled to a thrashing ground, where the valuable grain was cleaned by flailing or some other means.[2]

As summer wore on, cornfield beans ripened and were picked and dried in the sun. Some of the greenest were left in the hulls to be threaded on a string and hung out to dry into leather-britches for keeping until needed during the winter.[3] In late summer's sultry dog days the corn and tobacco crops were finally made. The ears of corn were picked and hauled to the corn crib to await gay corn-shucking events. No such gaiety was involved, however, in harvesting the tobacco, just hard heavy work. Tobacco plants were cut off at the ground, gathered, hauled, lugged, and hung from poles in the barns and sheds to dry.

The last summer days and the early ones of fall saw the good folk of the Valley harvesting pumpkins, squash, beans, potatoes, apples, cherries, peaches, plums, sorghum cane, and a host of other fruits and vegetables. The cane would be cut and stacked, soon to be made into molasses. And of course the fruits would be either dried for preservation or rendered into delicious jams, jellies, and ciders. The dark, cool cellars and barn corners were used as hiding places for apples and potatoes. There they were packed away in beds of earth and straw to keep from spoiling and to be dug out when needed in the cold months to come.

Yes, the Pigeon Valley summers long ago were indeed a time for growing and cultivating, which meant long hard days of work for the people who lived there. Yet slaving and toiling in the fields were not the only matters of concern for those dauntless highlanders. Their lives were richer and more diverse than might be expected. Looking back, it's possible to imagine their summer as a time when . . .

- *the cool waters of the nearby river or creeks lure young boys and girls from the fields to take a dip before hoeing another row*

- *deep, low rumbles of thunder announce the entry of threatening dark clouds into the Valley and incite the sudden afternoon showers that were soon to follow*

• the berries in the high fields ripen in the sun, and anxious boys and girls join together for day-long gathering excursions and oftentimes a little courting to boot

• the little cabins are infernos, with the sun bearing down and the hearth fire under the skillet or kettle still burning, and the young'uns soon seek escape in the shady woods

• women and girls stir dirty, perspiration-soaked clothes in kettles of boiling water with their "battling" sticks

• rustic wooden sleds towed by four-legged critters haul loads of corn or fodder or fruit off the hill or out of the bottom

• bodies rise early to start the coffee boiling, cornbread baking, and ham frying over the hot ashes of the hearth

• the bees, working feverishly among the late-blooming sourwood trees, fill the mountaineers' hollowed-out log gums with their delicious sourwood honey

• biscuits and cornbread slathered with sourwood honey or molasses is the most delicious eating there is

• bare feet are as tough as nails and seemingly impervious to prickly thorns and the rocks and clods in the fields

• the shirtless and perspiring blacksmith labors mightily between a hot forge and anvil, hammering and beating while children and other onlookers hover and bend his ears with ceaseless chatter

• the aroma of apples cooking in great kettles wafts tantalizingly across the fields, giving pause to the work of exhausted men and children

• a young boy might be entrusted to carry the last sack of the previous year's corn over to the mill for a turn

• women tend to house gardens planted in beans, pepper, squash, potatoes, and other vegetables while the baby lies in sight, wiggling or sleeping on a quilt

• patches of cotton or flax grow near many houses and come wintertime will keep the womenfolk gainfully occupied over spinning wheels and looms

• free time, and opportunities to go loafer and chaw with the boys over at Cathey's store, are rare

• a body must take great caution when wading through the blackberry brambles and keep an eye and ear open for rattlesnakes

• after the crops are laid by, entire families pack up and head off to join their neighbors at camp grounds where they will hear the Good Word from sunup till sundown for a week or more at a time

• rainy days bring respite for the farmers as they gaze across the fields from their shelters at the weeds growing taller and taller

• in the late afternoons young boys might be allowed to go off and catch some supper at a favorite fishing hole

• in the heat of summer the privy smells worse than ever, and folk don't tarry long there

• the blistering heat of the day dissipates quickly in the late evening hours, making the airy cabins more tolerable for sleeping

• apples and peaches are peeled, pared, and laid out on rooftops to dry in the sun

• the men and children tramp into the house after a hard day's work to find a delicious apple pie covered with sourwood honey as their just reward

• young girls and boys traipse for the stock shed in the early morning hours to milk the old cow

• milk, clabber, and butter are stored in quenching baths of cool spring water to keep

• overflowing corn cribs and grain bins make a body proud and content

• the sultry days of late summer mean that the crisp days and deep blue skies of fall are just around the corner.

Much like today, summertime in the Pigeon Valley many years ago was sunny, hot, and sultry in the daytime while the evening temperatures were a good bit cooler and not unpleasant. Sudden, violent thunderstorms were common as well, and were usually welcomed for their hydrating effect on the crops. Summertime presented these favorable conditions, enabling the early Valley farmers to produce and to survive—to grow their crops and their families, and to grow opportunities to improve their circumstances.

Opposite: Carroll Jones (left) and younger brother, Rego, pose in their Sunday finest in Canton during the 1950s. (Collection of the author.)

11 Reminiscences of a Canton Boy

CANTON, NORTH CAROLINA, IN THE 1950S AND '60S was a small, progressive town lying along the Pigeon River in Haywood County. It was built up around Champion's huge paper mill beside the river and straddled an important railroad artery and turnpike running through the mountains. At that time, before the advent of shopping malls, huge chain discount stores, and medical centers, Canton's city streets thrived with small retail and service businesses and professional offices.

These enterprises supported the needs and commerce generated by local factory workers, Pigeon Valley farmers, and tourists visiting the mountains. Commercial activity centered primarily along Main and Park and the few streets interconnecting them. Closely surrounding the compact business district, and mostly within walking distance, were the churches, elementary schools, high school, and residential neighborhoods.

It was not much more than that—just a little incorporated village tucked away in the mountains and populated with friendly working-class citizens. I was once one of those citizens, having been born and raised in Canton during the above-mentioned period. Although more than twenty-five years removed now, I still consider Canton my hometown and the residence of a goodly portion of my life's memories.

Most of these recollections are pleasant, with a few bittersweet ones mixed in for good measure. Unpleasant or outright unhappy experiences have been excised, for the most part, as the years have flown by and time has marched relentlessly on. Often, when I reminisce on those youthful days, Canton seems to take on an idyllic, almost Mayberrylike fantasy. Of course I know that it is not so. These fleeting dreams always evaporate upon further reflection and the realization that Canton was just an ordinary small town like so many thousands of others spread throughout the country.

But of course the history of every place is made up of our collective experiences and memories. If we don't record these remembrances before they fade away, our history is lost to us; if we do, we are all the richer for it. With that in mind I have taken the opportunity to put down these most recent hometown reminiscences.

* * *

Perhaps more than any other institution, our schools are what identify us as communities. I remember walking back and forth to Pennsylvania Avenue School across the old iron bridge (from which Canton took its name back in 1895[1]) spanning the Pigeon River and making the arduous hike up Mears Avenue, or better known to us at the time as "Steep Street." Along the way we passed in front of the pool hall at the corner of Main and Steep Streets. Mother had warned us about that place and forbade us to ever enter, so we would customarily hurry by its front after casting a wary eye through the large window to glimpse its dark interior. As we entered the Penn Avenue school building our senses were immediately stung with the peculiar and familiar odor of the slick, oil-soaked floors and the darkness of the hallways. Those floors were perfect for sliding in our school shoes, and it was all we could do to resist the urge to take off running and have a good skid. Classroom time was punctuated by milk breaks, occasional fire drills, and lunch in the cafeteria. Recess periods were anxiously awaited, and at the bell's clamor throngs of classmates rushed to the playground to climb the old swing-set supports (the swings had long ago disappeared) and play under the canopy of huge oak trees.

Select students were chosen daily to dust the chalk board erasers outside, usually against the trunks of the numerous trees around the school. For those daring scholars who chose to slap the erasers against the side of the brick building the punitive measures could be quite severe. School days brought the bad as well as the good, as I remember. I can recall stressful trips to the Health Department situated above the old jail to get shots and polio vaccinations. On the lighter side, trips to the new Canton Library next to the post office were pleasurable excursions. Mrs. Avery, the librarian, was always helpful and ready to offer suggestions for the best reading material and eager to sign us up for her next reading program.

Grammar school comprised grades one through six. After those formative years I attended the seventh and eighth grades at Canton Junior High and then Canton High for the first two years of high school and Pisgah High the last two. Football, basketball, baseball, and golf were passions that consumed a goodly portion of my time and attention throughout the high school years. Those pursuits provided to me the good fortune of playing on teams coached by Boyd Allen, Bill Stamey, Bob Holcombe, Bill Churm, Scott Connor, and other highly capable men. During the summers in high school and college I worked for my first employer, the Town of Canton, lifeguarding, cleaning streets, cutting grass, umpiring baseball games, and collecting garbage.

Downtown Canton was a busy place back then because, prior to construction of Interstate 40, all east-west traffic through the region was routed into Canton's downtown area. Main Street and Park Street had two-way traffic, and the Trailways bus station located next to the Colonial Theatre on Park Street was a bustling commuter hub. I can easily recall many of Canton's buildings and retail establishments from my youthful years. We shopped with Mother at the dime store for toys, Western Auto for bicycles and sleds, Jack Feingold's Army Store for PF Flyer tennis shoes and dungarees, or Winters' Department Store for finer church apparel. By far the best shopping experiences of all, perhaps, were those spent prowling the aisles and shelves of Stone's Paint and Wallpaper Store for ball gloves, bats, cleats, and all manner of other sports equipment.

We also accompanied Mother on her frequent procurement

trips to the old and new Smathers' Market grocery stores and eavesdropped as she visited with Loranzo Smathers, the proprietor, and his other customers. I remember Mom and Dad buying gas at Gregory's Esso Station and hearing them tell Marjorie Gregory to "charge it" after her husband, Ed, had checked under the hood. For some reason Dad always seemed to prefer Dodge automobiles back then, but I recall more clearly admiring the latest shiny models at Murphy's Chevrolet on Main Street and the Ford dealership on Park.

Several places in town offered opportunities for youngsters or the family to enjoy themselves. We might have a Coke in the soda shop under Dr. Wells's second-floor dental office at the corner of Main and Park Streets, squeezing into those tiny tables and chairs. Or we could go to Charlie's Restaurant after church for a hot dog and a Grapette soft drink. On rarer occasions, I remember going to Charlie's for a milk shake as a reward for hitting a home run. Because downtown was within easy walking distance from our home on Pearl Street we kids often hiked to the Colonial Theatre to see movies like *Old Yeller* and *Davy Crockett* and too many westerns to count. Although strongly averse to dancing for most of my youth, I warmly recall experiences clogging with the "Y" team in front of real live audiences who were appreciative of this unique form of dancing styled by our Scots-Irish ancestors generations before. And on Saturday nights young girls and boys could attend "sock hops" at the YMCA gym, and I recollect sitting along the wall at those affairs listening to the records and waiting to see if one of the girls might ask me to dance.

The imposing red-brick Champion YMCA edifice was squeezed into a site immediately adjacent to the paper mill and next to the Southern Railway yard. It was the hub of youth sports and social activities in Canton, and was the primary venue where we learned to swim under the watchful eye of Paul Rogers and played basketball in a "crackerbox" gym, learning to thread long set shots through the roof trusses. However, in the early 1960s the old structure was demolished to make room for Champion Papers' growing footprint. During the brief interim when the new Robertson Memorial YMCA was being constructed I can recall that a temporary "Y" was established in an existing store building next to Sluder's Furniture Store.

The "Y" sponsored the town's Little League Baseball program. Boys played Farm League, Little League, and Senior Little League ball for managers like Barton Ray, Claude Ford, and Tony Jones. We also played football and basketball for the Canton "Y" mite and midget teams with German ("Nazi") Miller and George Price running the show. Football practices were held on the field across from Charlie's Restaurant (at the location of the future Robertson Memorial YMCA), and at the end of each practice session we ran laps around the horse show ring that was located there, huffing and puffing and complaining all the way.

All of the youth sports programs in those days required a certain level of funding. It seemed that Nazi, who worked for the "Y," was always organizing drives to raise money, which usually amounted to his dispersing all the town's young athletes on sales campaigns throughout the residential neighborhoods and commercial district. I

The Champion YMCA served as a community center for social and athletic activities in Canton, North Carolina, during the 1950s. It provided organized programs for youth sports and was a popular venue for swimming, basketball, meetings, dances, and banquets, among other uses. This building was demolished in the 1960s to make way for an expansion of Champion's paper mill. (Collection of the author.)

can remember selling peanuts, popcorn, Christmas wrapping paper and cards, and concessions. And I have a vivid memory of selling Christmas trees on Park Street during the cold December days and nights and taking refuge in Nazi's little heated shack.

Summer in a river town was always a time for recreation in the water. After buying fishhooks and sinkers at Bill Schull's Nantahala Hardware Store and digging a can full of red worms, we would wade and fish the Pigeon River all the summer day long. I remember fishing off of the town's Park Street and Main Street bridges, too. Our catches would usually include bream, red-eyed bass, hornyheads, silversides, and hogsuckers, which we particularly despised. Tubing down the Pigeon River was another popular summer diversion, as was swimming at the Canton Recreation Park, where we relished the chance to dive off the high board. Many were the times, also, when my brother and I played golf from dawn until dark at the nine-hole Mountain View Golf Course with our buddies. With them I climbed the mountain behind our house on Pearl Street to stand on top of the town's reservoir and look down on the good folk of Canton. It was a view both comforting and inspiring, a view at once of home and a much larger world surrounding it.

I recall going to summer camp at the YMCA's Camp Hope and the many fun things associated with that experience—staying up late for nighttime campfires and storytelling, sleeping in squeaky bunk beds inside rustic cabins, learning archery, making crafts, swimming in the cold, cold East Fork River, and making new friends. Those blissful experiences are perfectly counterbalanced with my memories of high school football camp at Camp Hope and how much fun that was *not!*

Hot, sultry Friday and Saturday nights in Canton always included Champion "Y" fast-pitch softball games. Local players were idolized—men the likes of Nazi Miller and his brother, Clyde, George Price, Wade Garrett, Bill Bearden, Charlie Poindexter, Ron Peterson, Gus Colagerakis, Red Ivester, Jim Rhea, Bob Holcombe, Jackie Murdock, "Snake" Moore, and "Tow Head" Green. We kids alternated watching the men's games, chasing foul balls, and playing "cup" ball behind the bleachers where we tried to imitate our Champion "Y" heroes. I will never forget "Peaches Night" at the fast-pitch games, when the Spartanburg team would unload baskets of

During the 1950s large crowds thronged into Canton and lined the streets on Labor Day to watch the bands, floats, distinguished citizens, politicians, fire trucks, and horseback riders parade by. (Collection of the author.)

peaches from their station wagons between games and pass out the delicious fruit to all the fans.

Labor Day marked the end of summer, with swimming, diving, and archery contests at the Recreation Park and a traveling carnival that was usually set up in the field behind the National Guard Armory. I remember standing on the Park Street bridge amid throngs of local citizenry cheering and admiring as local high school bands, majorettes, politicians, city officials, fire engines, National Guard troops, and horseback riders paraded through the town. I recall riding the rides and selling food, drinks, and cotton candy for Nazi's ball teams out of makeshift concession stands sheltered with paper-machine felts and heavy paper board. And I can certainly recall the real "labor day" when our Champion "Y" football team, toiling under Nazi's close supervision, cleaned up the mess left behind after the celebration was over and the rides had moved out.

Most memories, of course, revolve around family and home, and I have many of those that remind me of my loving parents and brother. The hearth in our home was an oil-burning furnace that sat in the kitchen/dining room and forced its smelly heat throughout the house during the cold mountain winters. A small black-and-white television set was the focal point of the living room, where my brother and I would flop down on the bare wooden floor to play games, hone budding artistic skills with crayons and coloring books, and watch cartoons. One small bathroom—with a tub but no shower—and two bedrooms completed the modest dwelling on Pearl Street where we lived for a time in my early years.

I will never forget waking one morning to find Dad in the kitchen with the oven door wide open and its coils red hot. On that occasion, when he had inadvertently let the fuel oil tank run dry, he was seated in front of our kitchen stove basking in the warmth it provided and enjoying his morning coffee and newspaper, as if nothing were amiss. And many were the mysterious, quiet mornings when we awoke to a new-fallen snow and watched as Dad donned an army coat, pulled on his old "bear-hair" hat, strapped on his boots, and trudged off on foot to work at the paper mill. Those were the mornings when we anxiously crowded around the radio or television and listened with hopeful ears to learn if the school day had been cancelled due to the snow. If that indeed was the case, then a day of sledding, building snowmen, eating snow cream, and at last exchanging wet clothes for clean, warm ones was in store for my brother and me, and poor Mom too.

The end of each day's adventure brought our family together. I still smell Daddy and that paper-mill odor he brought home with him, along with the pulp still clinging to his steel-toed shoes. Thoughts of Mom's delicious meals at our kitchen table and the affection she bestowed on us conjure a fondness and love for her that will never go away or be replaced. Our house on Pearl Street, though simple and unpretentious, was a comfortable home in a comfortable community—a community I was proud of then and still am today.

Opposite: Ragmop, c. 1952. (Collection of the author.)

12 Ragmop

A Story about a Boy and His Dog

When I was a young boy growing up in Canton, North Carolina, in the 1950s, my mother used to say that Ragmop was the smartest dog she ever saw. "Why, once that dog saved your life!" she liked to tell me. Mom was referring to the time when I escaped the playpen and wandered beyond the yard surrounding the garage apartment where we lived, managing to crawl all the way out into the street. "Ragmop pitched the biggest barking fit you ever saw," she would say, "and came running hard as she could up those steps to the door to warn me that something was wrong." Ragmop was a "her" although I always thought of her as a "him." Having been alerted to the pending danger, Mom rushed out to the unpaved roadway where her wayward diaper-clad son had wandered and instantly removed me from harm's way. Pearl Street wasn't a very busy road then, nor is it now for that matter. But there was the occasional car that passed by, and you just never know what might have happened had it not been for Ragmop. Anyway, that's the way I remember the story. The thought of Ragmop actually being my savior was always lodged in the back of my mind as I was growing up, and along with it a certain degree of reverence.

But there is another story about Ragmop that I also have vivid memories of, and its veracity I can vouch for. It is the time when a young boy carried his dog off a high mountaintop back to civilization and to safety. The following is an account of this extraordinary adventure which seemingly takes on more and more peril as the years waft by.

* * *

"Don't walk out there," I hollered to my brother, Rego, and my cousin Doby. "See how the concrete is all broken and cracked? It could cave in with you and kill you." Mother had always warned us away from the huge concrete tank sitting on top of the mountain behind our house. The water reservoir had been built many years before to store and supply water to the town of Canton. We could see the reservoir easily from our house on Pearl Street. To all of us growing up at the foot of the mountain that huge tank reminded us of a castle jutting up into the clouds and commanding the whole valley along the Pigeon River, where Canton was situated. It was really just a hill but we always called it the "mountain." To get up to the reservoir required a good stiff hike. We would have to climb over, under, or through several barbed-wire fences and wade through pastures grown up with waist-high briars and patches of sumac. Ragmop had followed us up there that day and when we reached the top where

Ragmop looks on approvingly as Carroll Jones (left) and brother Rego pose for the camera on game day. (Collection of the author.)

the reservoir was situated he was panting hard, his tongue hanging out almost to the ground. I must have been about ten years old at the time which would have made Ragmop around twelve, or well into old age as far as dogs are concerned.

It was easy to climb up on top of the concrete reservoir. The tank was built into the hillside in a manner that allowed us to jump from the top strand of a barbed-wire fence and grab hold of the edge of the tank top. From there it was easy to pull ourselves the rest of the way up. Once on top it was just a huge expanse of flat concrete slab which had not weathered the years very well. The concrete was cracked and spalling badly, which made us ever mindful of Mom's warning. However, we were still young boys and on top of the world, so to speak, and felt no fears.

"Stay close to the edge and we'll be okay," I cautioned Rego and Doby as we walked around to get a good view of Canton from the north side of the reservoir. There were no guard rails, and on that side we must have been about thirty feet off the ground, or at least it seemed that high to me. I loved being up there unrestrained and reckless on the edge of that precipice and dreaming of making a perfect jackknife or swan dive. We could look down on the whole town and the sprawling Champion paper mill, partially hidden under clouds of vapor and black smoke rising into the air. That was in the days before environmental controls and equipment were installed on the boilers and other measures taken to prevent harmful emissions and discharges from the giant paper manufacturing facility. Little could I have suspected then that future events would present to me an opportunity to lead a great engineering and construction project that would further improve the mill's environmental performance, clean up the river, and breathe life into that old facility. But of course in those days we were blissfully ignorant of the dire consequences of industrial pollution as we looked on in wonder at the belching and spewing monster where Dad worked.

"Careful, Rego. Come over here by me." Rego was a little over a year younger than me but we were always close. He got a late start growing and I liked to believe that I had to look after my little brother.

"Where's Ragmop?" he asked.

"Probably resting somewhere," I offered, and then turning to Doby, asked, "What do you think of the view, Doby?" Larry Douglas Holbrook, better known as Doby after the famous Negro League ballplayer of the same name, was our first cousin—our mothers being sisters and all. Doby was a good athlete, just like his mother, Mildred, who was a star basketball player at Bethel High School. Although he lived over in Enka my dad had recruited him to play on our Little League baseball team—the Y's Men. So that summer we got to see a lot of Doby.

"Wow, look at all the smoke." Doby answered as he crept closer to the edge and pointed toward the mill. "Hey look, you can see the "Y" from here. Man, it looks so small," he went on. The "Y" that Doby was referring to was the Champion YMCA. To every young boy growing up in that era the Champion YMCA was synonymous with playing any kind of ball and it was a very important part of our lives.

"Looks like they're already fixing up the ball field for today's game," Rego added. It must have been an off day for the Y's Men, otherwise we would not have been climbing mountains and reservoirs and expending all of our energy. Swimming wasn't allowed, either, on game days. Mom and Dad were strict about that and always taught us how to prepare and stay focused on sports, school, and all our other pursuits. Thinking back on those days, I believe that we would rather have played baseball than anything else on earth.

"Hey Ragmop! How you doing, boy?" Rego yelled. "There he is, Carroll, over there under that tree." Looking down and toward the side of the reservoir where we had climbed up I saw Ragmop stretched out on his belly under a large oak tree anxiously staring back. He wasn't panting any more and was probably worried about us messing around on top of that reservoir where we had no business being. Hot days were especially tough on old Ragmop. I'm not real sure what kind of dog he was but would guess that his bloodlines were heavily mixed generations before. Covered with black and white shaggy hair, he looked all the world like a mop made of rags, and seemed much better adapted for arctic weather than the hot, sultry summer days of western North Carolina. I can recall that it was the funniest thing in the world when Mom used to give Ragmop a haircut. He looked so skinny and just like a plucked chicken. Rego and I would laugh and laugh at that poor little fellow after he got a shearing.

We jumped down off the reservoir and slid down a dirt embankment to get to the tree Ragmop had adopted. Taking great care to miss all the fresh cow piles lying around all over the place, we fell in with him on the ground to rest. The cows liked to cool off in the damp shady spots around the trees and especially enjoyed the rich, verdant grasses which were so tasty to them and grew best under the protective screening that the trees offered.

"Hey there, boy. Feeling better?" Rego asked with concern as he reached out and petted and scratched Ragmop's head.

We lounged there for a while in the dappled light under the spreading limbs of that oak tree, all stretched out on our backs looking up through the leaves for glimpses of squirrels and other signs of wildlife. The sun was almost directly overhead and darts and specks of sunlight penetrated the lush canopy. It was early summer and the small leaves were of a light green color and still growing. In some few places clusters of golden oak blossom tassels continued to hang, valiantly defying Mother Nature's design and even gravity. Off in the distance we heard J. C. Smathers's cows mooing at each other and the faint sound of a cowbell dangling from some unlucky one's neck.

"Who we playing tomorrow?" Doby suddenly blurted out.

"The Moose, and Daddy says that he bets they will pitch Benny Ford against us," I answered. Dad was our team's assistant manager, helping Barton Ray as needed and adding a lot of organization to the whole affair. He sure was good at that. It seems that about anything Daddy did, he went at it whole hog and was successful doing it. He and Barton even fashioned a large metal display board with a baseball diamond painted on it and used magnets painted as players to teach us the finer points of the game. As the team huddled around that board Daddy or Barton would create different game situations and say something like, "Okay, Carroll, there is one out, runners on second and third, here, and here," as they pointed to the board and player magnets. "If a sharp ground ball is hit to you at short what are you going to do with it?" That's how we learned the fundamentals of the game, and it demonstrates the kind of extra effort that those two men contributed and why we thought they were the best managers around.

"We'll beat him this time. Just you wait and see. I'd rather hit against a lefty any day and all you got to do against him is get the bat on the ball and it's going over the fence. Man, I can't wait to get up there and face him," Doby said confidently.

He was so confident that I didn't want to say anything that might dampen his enthusiasm or cast a little uncertainty over the spell he was under. But inside of me all I could think about was my being a left-handed batter and how I would rather face anybody else in the league but Benny Ford. After all, I was just ten years old and had been brought up to the Little League a year early. Heck, I was still trying to learn how to hit breaking pitches, and Benny Ford had a mean curve that dropped just as you started to swing. Later on in high school we would call that pitch a slider, but in the Little League it was just a mean curve.

"Hey, Doby. Do you want to use my Mickey Mantle?" Rego asked, and added, "I bet you can get it around better, but you better not break it." That was pretty generous of Rego. He had just gotten that new twenty-nine-ounce bat. Somebody else had borrowed and broken his old one, and when Mom saw him trying to fix it with nails and electrical tape she carried him over to Stone's Paint and Wallpaper and let him pick out a new one. She and Dad were good like that. They may not have been the richest folks in town, but you can be sure that we never wanted for school supplies or sports equipment or other necessities. And if one of our friends or teammates didn't have a glove or tennis shoes or needed a ride to the ballpark it wouldn't be long, either, before those situations were remedied.

Rego had not reached the Little League level yet. He was still in the Farm League, where he also played for the Y's Men team. It was either that year or the next when Rego accomplished the rarest of feats in baseball—he pitched a perfect game! Can you believe it? Never mind that it was the Farm League. Anybody who throws a perfect game has done something very special, buddy. Rego gained some notoriety for that amazing feat. He got his name in the local Canton and Waynesville papers, and everybody was making a big commotion over it. I believe Mom and Dad and I were prouder of Rego than he was of himself. It sure was something special for all of us, not just Rego, and I'll never forget that perfect game of his.

"Nah. I'll just stick with Louis Vetoe's Louisville Slugger. Don't worry. I'll get it around on him. Thanks anyway though," Doby replied.

"Hey, let's walk out that way through those woods," I volunteered. "There's a spring out there a little ways, somewhere, and we can let Ragmop get a drink of water."

"Are you thirsty, Raggie?" asked Rego as he petted and scratched Ragmop's head. That's what we always did—petted and scratched Ragmop's head and ruffled his fur.

"Yeah, let's go. I'll lead but you'll have to tell me the way," Doby said as he hopped up and off the ground.

Soon we were off hiking in a westerly direction along a low ridge rising ever so gradually and further and further away from Pearl Street. As I think back at that decision to keep on walking out through those woods with old Ragmop tagging along behind the crazier it seems to me. Not one of my better decisions for sure, but we were young and I knew those woods well and figured I knew where we were going. They were pretty woods. You know, the kind that is full of hardwood trees, not old, scraggly pines, and where the sunlight only filters through occasionally and the ground is carpeted with a thick litter of leaves and moss. The kind of quiet woods where you could dream of sneaking up and surprising a deer or a bear or wildcat or something. Of course we never saw any of those creatures up there on the mountain—just some of J. C. Smathers's old cows and maybe a possum or coon or box turtle every once in awhile. Weren't many snakes around back then, either, or at least we didn't see many, just a few black snakes. However, we forever remained vigilant and kept our eyes open because we knew there was a mean rattlesnake up there somewhere just waiting to get us.

There weren't any Indians around either, of course. They had all been chased out of the Pigeon Valley back in the late 1700s as the white man encroached into their mountain homelands. But back when I was growing up, cowboys and Indians and Davy Crockett were the rage. Seems like that is all we ever watched on TV, and we would walk over to town almost every weekend to see a new western movie at the Colonial Theatre. Man, I wanted one of those Davy Crockett coonskin hats real bad for a while—and a horse too.

Yeah, we thought about Indians a lot for sure. It was a habit of mine when I climbed around up there on the mountain to make a spear and carry it with me as I explored through those dark forests. The easiest way to make a spear, I found, was to break off a young sapling just above the ground and use my army knife to fashion the end into a sharp point. It wasn't as easy as all that, though, because my army knife was never very sharp and it took an effort to clean up the broken and frayed big end of the stick and sharpen a good point. I practiced throwing those spears at imaginary wild beasts and enemies that always seemed to take the form of trees. If the spear ever actually stuck in the tree and stayed without falling then I had "kilt the bear." The best trees to get "kilt" were dead trees, the ones that were decayed and would allow the spear point to penetrate and bury deep into the wood. It was a good feeling to kill those dead trees back when I was growing up.

Never mind looking for arrowheads up there on the mountain either. Certainly I knew, even at that young age, that the best places to find Indian artifacts were the fertile river and creek bottoms where their Indian villages and camps had been located. But even that insight didn't dampen my enthusiastic curiosity, and you can rest assured that my eyes were always peeled to the ground looking for a familiar shape or the glint of quartz or flint.

"The spring is down there," I said pointing down the north face of the slope. We had been walking for the better part of an hour since starting out from the reservoir. "It's in that gully right over there under that big rock. See where all those laurel bushes are growing—it's right in there." I'm not too sure if they were laurels or rhododendrons. Back then I didn't know the difference and still today have a hard time recognizing which is which. I had only been to that spot once before when I was with another older cousin, and I don't know how he found out about the spring. This was the furthest on the mountain that I had ever ventured and I was sure proud of myself for finding that spring. But Ragmop was breathing hard again and not looking too spry.

"Hey, Carroll, Ragmop's in bad shape. Do you think we ought to let him rest here?" Rego asked, and I could tell he was worried about Ragmop.

"Let's take him down to the spring so he can get a drink," I said. "I'll carry him."

"Here, I'll get him," Doby said as he reached down and picked up Ragmop. "Let's go."

When we got down there to the gully where a huge rock cropped out of the mountain side, we found the bank leading to the spring to be a bit steeper than it looked. All of a sudden, as we were tentatively negotiating our way down, Doby lost his traction and began to slide down on his backside, feet first.

"Woooooaaaa...........Watch *outtttt!"* he hollered as he landed hard in the wet seepage around the spring. He kept hold of Ragmop the whole time he was falling that last ten feet or so and never let him drop. We held our breath for a moment until Doby let Ragmop loose on the ground and started laughing. And when we saw that he was okay we started breathing easier and burst out laughing with him, more relieved than tickled.

"Boy, that was fun," he said. "I'll have to try it again." But I don't think he really wanted to try it again. He could have gotten hurt real bad and we all knew how lucky he had been.

"Yeah, right," I said. "You did good, holding on to Ragmop, Doby—real good. Thanks!"

"That was the only thing I could think about," Doby replied. "Didn't want old Raggie to get hurt," he continued as he felt around with his hand for a sore spot on his butt and fooled with his britches. "Dag-nab-it, I tore my dungarees! Look! See! Think Aunt Jimmie can patch them up for me?" he whined.

"Hey, look," Rego chimed in as he pointed toward Ragmop, who had already found the cool sweet spring water and was lapping it up as fast as he could. "Ragmop sure was thirsty—weren't you, boy?"

What a beautiful little place we had found up there at that high spring on the mountain. It was hard to believe that there was water coming out of the ground so high up, but it was and there was a pretty good flow too. Cupping our hands together we dipped them into the little pool of water and drank our bellies full. Never tasted better water, I remember thinking. There was no telling how long that big gully had been in the making, I thought as I studied our surroundings. It probably got started just after the timber was cut off the mountain in the late 1800s by a big timber company or, possibly, in the early 1900s for pulpwood. Canton and Clyde were booming about that time in consequence of the railroad's arrival to those remote towns in about 1882 and the construction of a huge pulp mill in Canton just after the turn of the twentieth century.

Over the years as thousands of "gully-washer" rains fell and ran off down the mountain, and with no tree roots to secure the ground, the topsoil would have been gradually eroded and scoured away around the exposed rock formation. The huge rock resisted these forces and was left in place as a growing gully was formed around and below it where we found our little spring oasis. It didn't appear that cattle had been using the spring or the land for some time. The old pastures surrounding it had grown up in thistle and stunted trees, and there was some fencing still evident but mostly fallen down, rusted, and broken. We stayed there at that cool little refuge for a half hour or more and until we noticed that the sun had moved way further over into the afternoon region of the sky.

Ragmop was all rested up again and appeared to be perky and in pretty good shape. I carried him this time as we climbed out of that spring gully and scrambled back up to the top of the ridge where we had first spied the spring. As mentioned before this was the limit of my previous explorations on the mountain. We could see that to the west, in the direction that we had been headed and where the sun was retreating, there loomed the steepest and highest mountain in the whole area. In the opposite direction, where we had come from, was mostly downhill and an easy walk for Ragmop now that he had been hydrated and rested.

That mountain in front of us that we had discovered—there was something ominous and tempting about it. Some mysterious force or forces seemed to be pulling and enticing us toward its precipitous slope. One could make the stretch to compare these influences with those that lured the pioneers westward—the spirit of adventure, a desire to see unknown territory, a hunger for new farmland, and the challenge of getting there. Surely those same motives (except that we weren't seeking land, of course) contributed to our fateful decision to keep plodding on and attempting to scale that high peak. But probably more than anything else adolescent innocence and naiveté were to blame. And as I think back on the occasion it seems likely that it was really my crazy idea to keep going; but Rego and Doby wanted to climb that high mountain as bad as I did and neither expressed any feelings of uncertainty about marching onward.

Never had I seen such a steep mountain—so steep that we worried about falling over backward and all the way back down to the bottom. No, I am not kidding, it was that steep. And it was a brutal interminable climb to the top. Ragmop gave out early in the climb and just lay down, looking at us with those big black pitiful eyes. Doby and I took turns toting him. The one carrying the dog had to go first as the others followed close behind to prop and keep him and Ragmop from falling over backward.

About halfway up that steep mountain face we came across a few man-made depressions in the hillside that looked like old caves that might have collapsed many years ago and silted up. Stopping to investigate, we detected that all around the area were large pieces or flakes of mica. It wasn't unusual to see pieces of mica in the mountains—you could find mica about anywhere. But this was a little out of the norm. There was more of it here, and the pieces were bigger and strewn everywhere. It didn't occur to me then that those holes in the ground could be the remnants of a mica mining industry that flourished in the area many years before. Mica was used to make all manner of things, including electron tubes, radio capacitors, and lenses for goggles, and was a much sought-after mineral during the World Wars. As I grew older I remembered those holes and what we had seen that day, and am now almost certain that we stumbled upon some old mica mines and just didn't realize it.

After nosing around those collapsed caves and resting a spell we continued our ascent and finally reached the summit. Gradually transitioning from climbing on all fours to a standing position, we slowly began to take in the panorama. The vista from that great vantage point was a wondrous thing to behold and an experience to treasure always. Here we were, three boys and a dog, standing on top of the world where few men or women or dogs had ever set foot before. If you could combine the sensation of climbing Mount Everest and finding a lost civilization such as Peru's Machu Picchu, then that would describe very well how we felt. Although I don't remember doing it, I have no doubts that I spent a few moments looking around that ridge top for ancient walls or other clues to the previous culture that had existed there. What a feeling it was—and one never to be forgotten.

In every direction we could see forever, it seemed. The horizon that could barely be seen far off in the distance encircled us for 360 degrees and was defined by dark ragged mountains meeting the hazy blue late afternoon sky. To the north we looked down at the new four-lane highway linking Canton and Waynesville and could easily see the Midway Medical Center and bowling alley that stood alongside the roadway. In the opposite direction we could gaze out over Stamey Cove into the Pigeon Valley toward Bethel. As we looked to the west it was easy to discern that we were standing at the highest point of the mountain ridge line and could see that there was a hogback ridge falling away from us toward Clyde. And looking back from whence we had come, the reservoir could be seen way off in the

The top of "Reservoir Hill" offered a sweeping view of the Champion paper mill and downtown Canton, c. 1950s. (Collection of the author.)

distance and Canton and the Champion mill just beyond.

It was getting late and we were tired from the hard climb. After a few minutes the feeling of euphoria started to wear away and we began to assess our situation and determine the next move. The sun was getting to be very low in the sky by this time, and Rego and I both knew Mom was surely wondering where in the world we were. Ragmop was in no condition to walk and, no matter what, would have to be carried. If we backtracked the way we came, it would take us at least two hours to make it back home, and maybe not before dusky dark had set in. If we kept going ahead along the ridge leading toward Clyde there was no telling where that path might lead or how long it could take to find our way back to civilization. As we gazed down on the new highway and those Midway buildings in the far-off distance, another idea began to take form in our minds—one kind of out-of-the-box, but reasonable and logical and maybe even possible. And the notion offered a better chance of success, which translated to our getting home before dark, not getting lost or hurt, not making Mom worry too much, and above all taking care of Ragmop. I remember thinking about Ragmop more than anything else. We were not going to leave Ragmop behind! And we didn't.

We decided to make for the highway and the bowling alley. Shouldn't be too hard to slide back down that mountainside we had just conquered and walk off the north face of the ridge past the spring gully oasis and on down to the highway and the bowling alley at the foot of the mountain. It probably was no further than a couple of miles away, and we figured to make it in less than an hour's time. When we got to the bowling alley we could use the telephone to call Mom. We were three tired, hungry, and nervous young boys and a worn-out dog, and that is the plan that we hatched together. And I am happy to say it was a plan that we executed to perfection.

Mom didn't get mad at all. And we didn't even have to beg for forgiveness. She was overjoyed to hear my voice on the phone and I'll bet it didn't take her five minutes to get out there to Midway in the car to pick us up. I believe she was crying—no, I'm *sure* she was crying—and I remember all of us hugging and talking about how poor old Ragmop had to be carried off the mountain. Doby showed her the scrape on his rear end and the rip in his dungarees and asked hopefully if she could patch them for him. We were all excited and talking at the same time and telling Mom about our secret oasis and the old caves on the high mountain.

For the next day or two all concerns and worries were for Ragmop. He—or, rather, she—moped and limped around for a spell but gradually regained her strength and to our great joy returned to normal. Mom never stopped talking about how smart Ragmop was, either, and now she had another tale to tell. And I had another memory to go along with the one of Ragmop saving my life. In this one I was able to return the favor.

Opposite: A rustic "corn-cracking" mill was powered by water diverted from a swift-moving mountain stream. From Rebecca Harding Davis, "By-paths in the Mountains," *Harper's New Monthly Magazine* 61 (1880).

13 Plumb Proud of My Mountain Dialect

ALMOST IMMEDIATELY UPON ARRIVING on the campus of the University of South Carolina my freshman year, I began to notice something peculiar occurring. It seemed that the other students I conversed with, and even the coaches I engaged in dialogue, would cast curious grins back toward me. "Where're you from, anyway?" one of my new acquaintances would query, while another might remark, "Man, you talk funny. Say something else." So it was that I quickly came to realize upon that first venture outside the western North Carolina mountains to the capital city of Columbia, South Carolina, that there was something special about me that other people seemed to enjoy. A distinct mountain accent and dialect set me apart from everyone else and would eventually become a personal badge to proudly brandish as I grew into manhood and forged a life for myself beyond the mountains.

Living and growing up in Canton, North Carolina, in the 1950s and '60s and with roots firmly embedded in the Pigeon Valley, I acquired naturally the speech of my family, neighbors, and the local mountaineers without ever realizing or appreciating it. By that time more than one hundred and fifty years had passed since the first Indian traders and later Scots-Irish, English, and German settlers penetrated the remote mountain fastness of western North Carolina.[1] Over this time span their archaic dialect, which included vestiges of an Elizabethan language and employed a distinctive clipped speech, unusual colloquialisms, and concocted words and contractions, had been drastically watered down through a long evolutionary process.

Railroads, improved roads, and the timber industry opened up the vast Carolina highlands and brought the mountaineer farmers into more frequent contact with outsiders, or "furriners." The mountain farms themselves grew larger and began producing surplus grain crops and livestock that could be hauled and "drove" to faraway markets in Greenville and Charleston, South Carolina, and Augusta, Georgia, and later to nearby towns and rail hubs to be sold and bartered.[2] These commercial activities and other industries such as selling "sang" (ginseng), animal skins, and even distilled corn liquor began to gradually bring the mountain highlanders closer to the civilized folk and to have a profound influence on their culture and speech.

The Pigeon Valley region followed a somewhat similar progression. In the early days there were only a few farms lying along the Pigeon River where the rich, sandy soil was fertile and easily tilled. This choice land was claimed by those brave pioneers who arrived in the Valley first, likely finding the hearth fires of the retreating Cherokee Indians still warm. The vast majority of the settlers who followed found property along tributary streams and creeks and on the hillsides and ridges bordering these small watercourses. There they cleared away forests, constructed small log cabins, and hauled rock out of the fields in order to cultivate the land, feed themselves, and make a go of it in the wild, mountainous frontier.

As time went by and as generation succeeded generation, even these small enterprises began to prosper and to evolve into larger and more productive farms. Taken in aggregate, the output of surplus crops and livestock from the river farms and those smaller ones located in the hollers and perched on the hillsides began to stimulate the local economy. Demand for these surplus goods created an increasingly vigorous commerce between the Valley farmers and the nearby settlements, including Waynesville and the little hamlet of Pigeon River (Canton), and distant marketplaces such as Augusta. Later, in the time frame from the 1880s through about 1920, the arrival of the railroad, the onslaught of the timber barons, and the construction of a huge pulp mill in Canton further diversified the economy and provided for even more contact between the Pigeon Valley residents and the merchants, factory workers, and citizens of Canton, Clyde, and Waynesville.[3]

There is no doubt that this interaction with people considered to be outlanders, or outsiders, tended to dilute the old mountain dialect of my Pigeon Valley ancestors, but it didn't kill it outright. Horace Kephart, in his noteworthy study of the North Carolina mountaineers titled *Our Southern Highlanders*, promotes a belief that the mountain women were a primary reason that the unique dialect and speech of the highlanders persisted. From his perspective, living among the southern highlanders in the early 1900s, he observed that the mountain men traveled to the mills, villages, logging camps, and railroad towns regularly to trade and transact business, and tended to adapt their speech and habits to that of the outlander. On the other hand, domestic responsibilities of women prevented them from venturing beyond the surrounds of the tiny homesteads they inhabited. For this reason they remained insulated from the influence and infection of outsiders, and the integrity of their native dialect was preserved.[4] The faithful, dependable, and sturdy mountain women maintained much of the original mountain dialect for generations until schools and technological advances made it virtually impossible to remain completely isolated from the modern world.

However, there are still hints and strains of the mountain dialect left in our speech today and, as I first observed in my university days, they are still very noticeable to those who are not native to the Valley and unaccustomed to hearing it. My mother was born and raised in the heart of the Pigeon Valley, and her ancestry can be traced back to the first Hargroves, Shooks, Moores, and Catheys who began settling along the Pigeon River around 1800. Some of the colloquialisms and expressions she routinely used are so familiar to me today that I unconscientiously resort to them from time to time.

For example, if surprised or just plain perplexed with something, I might declare for everyone around me to hear, "Well, that beats a henaroot." The literal meaning of "henaroot" and the origins of this phrase have eluded me thus far, but I know how and when Mom used the expression to convey incredulity. So I tend to employ it occasionally under similar circumstances, to the puzzlement of my wife and delight of my daughters.

Another expression my mother sometimes used in an effort to add emphasis to an articulation was "bigger than Pete." "Why that man just up and left the country *bigger than Pete!*" she might have exclaimed. Although still not aware of the genesis of this idiom, I repeat it anyway from time to time to accent one of my utterances or simply to draw attention or extract a chuckle from an outlander.

By listening to and mimicking my parents and grandparents I have unwittingly acquired from them a treasure trove of dialect, colloquialisms, and words that are the remnants of the language spoken by their pioneer ancestors following the Revolutionary War. Some of the old mountain expressions and words that remain with us today come to mind readily, and I have listed below a sampling with my attempt to define them or add meaning. The reader will be left with these few in hopes that they stir memories and thoughts of others, and that they never be forgotten or go unspoken.[5]

- **afeared** afraid: "I ain't afeared of him."
- **airish** conceited or proud; derives from putting on airs: "That boy is a mite airish."
- **allow** think or figure: "Don't know what to allow about that kind of carrying-on."
- **battling paddle** a wooden paddle used to beat and

hammer the wash during the scalding and washing process: "She wielded a mean battling paddle on Monday wash days."

- **bodaciously** bodily or entirely: "I'm bodaciously hungry."
- **boomer** a type of mountain squirrel also known as a red squirrel or pine squirrel
- **carry** take: "I had to carry her over to town to see the Doc."
- **churched** getting kicked out of church for not living by the accepted standards and rules. Old-timers would get a couple of warnings before being "churched" for offenses such as drinking or not regularly attending church. This is an example of the mountaineers inventing a word because they didn't have another one that suited them. "Old John got churched for sampling the shine too much."
- **comeuppance** rude awakening: "A man that sips on ol' Jed's cider is in for a real comeuppance."
- **edzact** to cipher or figure out: "Let me study it over a spell and then I can edzact it."
- **fair-to-middlin'** about average; derives from a grading measure of the old cotton merchants: "I'm feeling fair-to-middlin' today."
- **feather into** attack; derives from the Old English expression of burying an arrow up to the feathers.

(Horace Kephart wrote that this expression was used long ago "before villainous saltpeter supplanted the long bow.") "She's fixin' to feather into him."

- **fetch** to get: "Go fetch the molassey sugar for Paw."
- **fixin'** getting ready: "I'm fixin' to pick a mess of collards."
- **fling** to throw: "He can fling a rock clear across the river."
- **hain't** has not or have not: "He hain't got no right to that land."
- **heerd** heard: "I ain't heerd hide nor hair of him again."
- **helve** the handle of a tool such as an ax or hammer: "Ain't nothing better than hickory for an ax helve."
- **hit** corruption of the pronoun "it": "Hit just ain't right, no ways."
- **holler** to yell: "He hollered so loud that they heerd him plumb over in the holler." Also another word for valley.
- **infare** a celebration or wedding feast put on by the groom's parents
- **josh** to kid or jest: "He's just joshing you."
- **laid by** put aside or put up or finish: "He's done got the crops laid by."
- **laid off** postponed; "I've laid off and laid off until I ain't got no choice now 'cept plow that field."
- **leather-britches** beans dried in the pod and then

boiled hull and all

- **lit out** set out or took off: "He lit out of here like a scalded dog."
- **mess** a quantity of one feeding of the family: "Let's string a mess of beans for tonight."
- **nare** or **nary** none or not any: "Ain't nary apple ain't got no worms." (This is also an example of a quadruple negative.)
- **peart** almost or near: "She's peart near finished with that thar quilt piece."
- **peckerwood** a woodpecker
- **plumb** all the way or completely: "Fill my poke plumb to the top."
- **plunder** junk: "Nothin' in that old shed 'cept a bunch of plunder."
- **poke** a paper bag or bag: "Fill up this here poke plumb to the top."
- **quair** odd, queer: "Ol' Jed sure has been acting quair here lately."
- **reckon** think or know: "I don't reckon I knowed him."
- **slut** makeshift candle made by filling saucer with fat and using a cotton cloth wick: "Better light up that slut to see by."
- **smidgen** a bit or morsel, more than a mite: "Give me a smidgen of tobaccer snuff."
- **stove up** jammed or jabbed: "He stove up his neck bad."

- **'tater and 'mater** potato and tomato: "We'uns going to have taters and maters with a mess of beans for dinner today."
- **tobaccer** tobacco: "Need to mosey over to Cathey's to get me some chaws of tobaccer."
- **toddick** from the term for the toll dish into which the miller measured his share of ground meal, a small measure or portion: "The miller earned his toddick today turning that wormy corn."
- **tol'able** tolerable or endurable: "She getting along tol'able well."
- **tote** carry: "Let's tote the corn over to the mill and get it run."
- **troublin' stick** the wooden stick or paddle used to stir the clothes when washing them in a kettle of boiling water and lye soap: "She troubled the water hard as can be with that troublin' stick of hern."
- **turn o' meal** turn; derives from the fact that each man had to wait his turn to have the meal ground at the mill: "It's his turn o' meal to work the roads."
- **yander** over there: "He's out yander in the field."
- **young'uns** young children: "Tend to the young'uns while I'm gone."
- **you'uns, we'uns** corruptions of the plural pronouns you and we: "Let's you'uns and we'uns jest saunter over thar and see what they allow."

Now that these old words and expressions are recorded, maybe they will survive a spell longer, to be taught to the young'uns growing up in the western mountains today. And don't be squeamish about using them on others, neither. Pity the first poor airish furriner that you josh—they'll reckon fur sure that they either heerd you wrong or edzact that you ain't got nary sense. Now if that don't beat a henaroot!

Opposite: The corn has been harvested and the stalks shocked in the field. (Farm Security Administration/Office of War Information Collection, Library of Congress.)

14 Autumn: A Time for Thanks

November in the mountains and the Pigeon Valley of western North Carolina, way back when, was indeed a time for the mountaineer farmers to be thankful. During the spring and summer hard work, keen wits, and the grace of God were enjoined to fullest advantage to coax grain crops from the rich bottomlands and the thin, rocky soils of the hillsides. By the time November came around, the corn and wheat had been harvested and the vegetables and fruit gathered and rendered into nutritional provisions to see the Valley's families through the long, cold winter ahead.

In November the men of the community would form up wagon trains loaded with their surplus production and livestock and make long droves to distant marketplaces in South Carolina and Georgia. At these foreign trade centers their yield was sold for scarce currency or bartered for other necessities that could not be grown or made at home. The mountaineers would return to the Valley and their small log cabins and anxious families with spending money jingling in their pockets and valuable provisions of coffee, salt, sugar, and other goods to see them through the hard months. Thus rewarded and with renewed hope and aspirations, the Valley farmers would count their blessings and be mighty thankful for their good fortune.

November in the Pigeon Valley also meant that cold weather had arrived and was fixin' to set in. I can picture those long-ago autumn seasons when . . .

- *the cribs are plumb full of precious maize*
- *autumn's brilliant red blazes and orange flames that once engulfed the trees are sadly extinguished, exposing forlorn, leafless skeletons bracing for the ravages of yet another winter*
- *the golden yellow burley hangs drying from sapling poles inside rustic little barns perched along creek banks and propped up on the hillsides*
- *ragged shocks of cornstalks and fodder stand in the fields, and pumpkins wait to be hauled to the barn*
- *long droves to faraway marketplaces take the menfolk from the family for many weeks at a time*
- *there is not much time left to squeeze the last of the cane cuttings and render their greenish-yellow juices into a golden molasses syrup*
- *corn shuckings allow young people to laugh and enjoy each other's company and perhaps win a buss from a sweetheart*

• farmers awaken in the mornings to find a glistening white rime blanket covering the highest knobs and lowest bottoms, and everything in between

• the woods and orchards are littered with chestnuts spilled from prickly burrs—and if a body didn't hurry with their tow sacks the ravenous foragers of the forest would find them first

• the gray squirrels are mighty fidgety, having lost their lofty leafy hiding places, and more alert to the perils of flying predators above and hunters sleuthing around below

• men gather and trek off into the woods to slay the wary ridge runners whose meat will sustain their families and their lives

• hog-killing and lye soap-making time entail hard yet essential work for the entire community

• young'uns pour bucket after bucket of water into the ash hopper to make lye water for soap making

• women boil and cook a pungent mixture of lye water and fat and pork and grease to render lye soap

• the smell of straw-covered apples and buried taters and cool earth fill the cellar or barn

• women stoop and stoke and stir huge boiling kettles of apples and cider and spices all day long to persuade its conversion to delicious apple butter

• farmers deliver their fresh shucked and shelled corn to the mill to be turned

• pumpkins overlooked in the field or still piled by the barn wear white caps of frost on a cold morning

• mouth-watering and belly-growling aromas mean that pumpkin bread and pumpkin butter and pumpkin pies are cooking on the stove and hearth

• families join in joyful evenings of banter and talk and corn popping before the warm hearth

• children return to school, wearing shoes, learning ciphers, and making friends

• the aroma of wood smoke fills the house and permeates the Valley

• axes fly, cutting firewood and chopping up kindling aplenty for the cook stove

• hog's meat hangs in the smokehouses, curing in the smoky fires

• young folks attend molasses-pulling affairs where romantic yearnings are stirred and sweethearts hope to get "stuck"

• crackling bread is made after the first hog killing

• snow on the mountain peaks and cold, gusting winds in the valleys stir the leaves and whistle through unfilled chinks in the logs

• mountain folk enjoy holiday feasts of pork and roast turkey, along with a mess of leather-britches beans, taters, corn bread, apple butter, pumpkin pie, milk, and cider

• grateful families say grace and give thanks for all of the above.

November meant all these things and much more to the early settlers of the Pigeon Valley. It was a time for being thankful, as we should be today for these memories and for the resilience and exertions of the Pigeon Valley ancestors before us.

Opposite: On the Lenoir homeplace, an old hearth and chimney stand, almost forgotten yet still vigilant today, over the East Fork of the Pigeon River. (Author's photo.)

Epilogue The Pigeon Valley Today

THE PIGEON VALLEY OF TODAY is not unlike the one presented to the readers of these pages. Although more densely populated for certain, the lands along the upper Pigeon River where the historic Forks of Pigeon community developed in the early 1800s still produce bountiful crops and still possess that rare pristine quality and beauty that is so swiftly disappearing in the modern world. The Valley is peopled with not only descendants of the pioneer families that first settled there, like the Catheys, Hargroves, Moores, Plotts, Lenoirs, Deavers, Edmondstons, and Blaylocks, but newcomers as well—all appreciative of the area's heritage and history and the richness of nature's gifts that surround them.

There are still churches and school buildings situated on or near the old sites selected by the early pioneers. Roads are far more numerous and most have been paved, straightened, and adapted for the horseless carriages of this era. However, the main road joining Waynesville and the Pigeon Valley through the Pigeon Gap still survives, coursing along an approximate route used not only by the early pioneer road builders but General Griffith Rutherford himself in 1776 on his punitive expedition against the Cherokee Indians. And there exists today a modern highway connecting the Pigeon Valley with Canton, which follows the old trace through "flowery garden," or the Garden Creek area. Local residents and travelers speed in automobiles over this important artery from the Forks of Pigeon environs to Canton in just a matter of minutes. Very few pause to reflect that once the trip was one of several hours by horseback or farm wagon over a roadway fashioned from sand, dirt, and rock and maintained by the citizenry of the community, as mandated by county law.

Vestiges remain of still another unpaved path that once led travelers along the back side of the river from Canton into the Pigeon Valley. This rutted old country road, sections of which can still be discerned to this day, paralleled the river along its banks and passed in close proximity to my grandmother's house. However, it, too, has been replaced by a two-lane asphalt road that runs just underneath the embankment where Granny Hargrove's house still presides over a fertile bottomland abutting the Pigeon River.

The Cathey store and mill, those centers of commerce in the Pigeon Valley in the years before and after the Civil War, are long gone and forgotten by most. Yet the stately old Cathey house stills stands sentinel-like near the site of the old store, as if waiting for the colonel himself to return home from a hard day's work at his busy mercantile enterprises. Unfortunately, William Burton Cathey's two-

A view across the Pigeon Valley from the Hargrove-Smathers farm in the 1950s, toward Cold Mountain in the distance. (Collection of the author.)

story frame house, built in about 1849 and host to young William Hargrove and his wife Nannie Cathey for a brief period after their marriage in 1869, has vanished in recent years. In its stead, signaling a growing and progressive Pigeon Valley community, is a beautiful, modern school building that has been constructed just to the south of Cathey Cove. There the future leaders of the community will begin their education and, just like Joseph Cathey, James and Etheldred Blaylock, William Hargrove, and other prominent Valley citizens before them, they will have to exert their energies and apply their intellectual powers to make the Pigeon Valley continue to bloom and prosper and support the changing lifestyles of its present-day inhabitants.

I hope the readers of this anthology have enjoyed their visit to the Pigeon Valley of days gone by. The early pioneers and settlers sacrificed much and survived unfathomable hardships to build a community called Forks of Pigeon. And some left behind footprints that preserve historic and authentic tales of their lives and deeds. Quite possibly, many readers of these pages will have caught a glimpse of their own heritage, as well, and discovered just how deep their roots run in the valley of Forks of Pigeon.

Notes

Prologue Forks of Pigeon in the Early Years

1. Ora Blackmun, *Western North Carolina: Its Mountains and Its People to 1880,* (Boone, N.C.: Appalachian Consortium Press, 1977). In the first several chapters the author makes an excellent presentation of the encroachment of white settlers into Cherokee Indian territories and the various treaties that were negotiated.

2. Kathy Ross, *Haywood History, 1809–Civil War* (Mountaineer Publishing Co., c. 2005).

3. W. Clark Medford, *Early History of Haywood County* (Asheville, N.C.: Miller Printing Co., 1961), pp. 20, 21.

4. Blackmun, p. 317.

5. Loralee Kendall Iglesias, "Colonel Joseph Cathey of Haywood County, North Carolina: Nineteenth Century Merchant, Entrepreneur, and Community Leader," unpublished thesis submitted Nov. 21, 2003, University of North Carolina at Asheville, p. 14.

6. Iglesias, pp. 16, 17.

7. Iglesias, pp. 17, 18.

8. W. Clark Medford, *Middle History of Haywood County* (Asheville, N.C.: Miller Printing Co., 1968), p. 66; (Waynesville, N.C.) *The Mountaineer,* Bicentennial edition, July 1976.

9. Medford, *Middle History,* pp. 67, 68.

10. Rev. Thomas Erwin, *Life Sketches of Thomas Erwin,* copy of unpublished and undated document in possession of author, p. 72. Haywood County Schools, *Haywood County Schoolin': A Rich Heritage,* c. 1991.

Chapter 1 Rutherford's Expedition

1. For a description of Gen. Rutherford's path into the mountains and general accounts of his actions against the Cherokee Indians see John Preston Arthur, *Western North Carolina: A History from 1730 to 1913* (Asheville, N.C.: Edward Buncombe Chapter of the Daughters of the American Revolution of Asheville, North Carolina, 1914 repr.

NOTES TO CH. 1, *continued*

Johnson City, Tenn.: Overmountain Press, 1996), pp. 55 and 379; Blackmun, *Western North Carolina,* pp. 109–14; Medford, *Early History*, pp. 1, 2; and Gaillard Tennent, "The Indian Path in Buncombe County," map [ind002], D. H. Ramsey Library, Special Collections, University of North Carolina at Asheville (originally published Asheville, N.C.: Stephens Press, n.d. [after 1950?]).

2. Medford, *Early History*, pp. 1, 2.

3. Medford, *Early History*, p. 37.

Chapter 3 CAPTAIN HACK

1. The undated newspaper clipping is in the author's possession.

2. Hargrove genealogy information was researched and recorded by Albert (Tony) C. Jones of Canton, North Carolina.

3. Rev. Thomas Erwin, *Life Sketches,* p. 75. Erwin wrote, "Augustus lived in Peter's Cove at the DeKalb Kinsland house that burned down."

4. William L. Barney, *The Making of a Confederate: Walter Lenoir's Civil War* (Oxford and New York: Oxford University Press, 2008), p. 29. Barney states that Augustus Hargrove was employed as the "overseer" on absentee plantation of Thomas Lenoir (father of Thomas Isaac Lenoir) on the East Fork of the Pigeon River in the mid-1840s. Lenoir Family Papers, Southern Historical Collection, University of North Carolina at Chapel Hill: Two letters from A. C. Hartgrove to Rufus T. Lenoir (brother to Thomas Isaac Lenoir) dated 12/29/1861 and 1/13/1862 report on the affairs of Thomas Isaac Lenoir's plantation on the East Fork of the Pigeon River. During this time Captain Thomas I. Lenoir was serving as captain of Haywood County's Company F of the 25th Regiment N.C. Infantry Troops, which was stationed at Grahamville, S.C.

5. Erwin, *Life Sketches*, p. 72; *Haywood County Schoolin',* p. 92.

6. W. C. Allen, *The Annals of Haywood County, North Carolina: Historical, Sociological, Biographical, and Genealogical* (1935; repr. Spartanburg, S.C.: Reprint Company, 1977), p. 148.

7. Carroll C. Jones, *The 25th North Carolina Troops in the Civil War: History and Roster of a Mountain-Bred Regiment* (Jefferson, N.C.: McFarland, 2009). Information regarding William Hartgrove's Civil

War record and that of the 25th Regiment N.C. Infantry Troops is taken from this work.

8. Allen, *Annals of Haywood County*, p. 148.

9. *Diary and Reminiscences of W. H. Hargrove,* privately printed Sweetwater, Tex., Dec. 1938, by Hattie Rue and Dale Campbell. Copy in possession of author is approximately 4" x 6" in size, has six pages, and is bound in heavy-weight silver-colored paper.

10. *Diary and Reminiscences of W. H. Hargrove.*

11. *Diary and Reminiscences of W. H. Hargrove.* Hartgrove identifies these "illegitimate influences" elsewhere as "newspapers of the day" and "big mouth politicians."

12. *Diary and Reminiscences of W. H. Hargrove.*

13. Medford, *Early History,* pp. 164–69.

14. William Hargrove's journal was given to the author by Nannie Hargrove Smathers, granddaughter of William Harrison Hargrove. It is approximately 4" x 6" in size and has forty-three existing pages that are in poor condition. The cover page has been torn from the binding and is loose. At the top of this page is written "Wm H. Hartgrove's Book". The pages are filled with William's handwritten notes and records in pencil and ink.

15. Jones, genealogy information.

16. Wm Hartgrove's Book.

17. *Diary and Reminiscences of W. H. Hargrove.*

18. *Diary and Reminiscences of W. H. Hargrove.*

19. *Diary and Reminiscences of W. H. Hargrove.*

20. *Diary and Reminiscences of W. H. Hargrove.*

21. Minutes of Haywood County Commissioners' Court, June 7, 1876.

22. "Capt. W. H. Hargrove Dead—Canton's First Citizen and Soldier Answers Last Roll Call," *Canton Vindicator,* Apr. 23, 1909. Hack Hargrove's obituary in part reads, "Along temperance lines he was without an equal. His life was devoted to this cause and he was ever on the alert in its interests. He was an active member of the Sons of Temperance, and at one time held the highest office in the state. Captain Hargrove's life was an open book as pure and clean as is possible for man to be."

23. Minutes of Haywood County Commissioners' Court, Dec. 2, 1878.

NOTES TO CH. 3, *continued*

24. "Haywood Has Enjoyed Four Courthouses," *The Mountaineer*, Bicentennial edition, July 1976.

25. Camille Wells, *Canton: The Architecture of Our Home Town* (Waynesville, N.C.: Mountaineer Graphics, 1985), pp. 22–25.

26. Minutes of Haywood County Commissioners' Court, book 2, Feb. 6, 1882.

27. Wells, *Canton*, pp. 22–25.

28. Minutes of Haywood County Commissioners' Court, book 2, p. 273, June 1885.

29. Minutes of Haywood County Commissioners' Court, book 2, p. 444, Dec. 4, 1888.

30. Allen, *Annals of Haywood County*, p. 148.

31. "Masons Influenced All Areas of Haywood County Development," *The Mountaineer*, Bicentennial Edition, July 1976.

32. A copy of one such survey, signed by W. H. Hartgrove and dated April 1897, in author's possession, records a division of land north of Canton that covers an area extending from the confluence of Beaverdam Creek and the Pigeon River on the south to the vicinity of the present day Interstate 40 highway on the north.

33. The newspaper clipping was found within the pages of an 1886 volume titled *Life and Campaigns of General Robert E. Lee* given to the author by Nannie Hargrove Smathers. A pencil inscription in the book identifies the owner as "W. B. Smathers, 1890". William Burton Smathers served in the Confederate army during the Civil War and fought along side Hack Hargrove in the ranks of the 25th Regiment North Carolina Infantry Troops.

34. Medford, *Middle History*, pp. 34, 35.

35. "Capt. W. H. Hargrove Dead – Canton's First Citizen and Soldier Answers Last Roll Call," *Canton Vindicator*, Apr. 23, 1909. Author obtained microfilm records of several old *Vindicator* editions from the North Carolina State Archives and Records.

36. "Capt. W. H. Hargrove Dead," *Canton Vindicator*, Apr. 23, 1909. "The death of Capt. W. H. Hargrove at the home of his son, J. A. Hargrove on Pigeon River, last Tuesday night at 10 o'clock, removes from our midst our first citizen, and Haywood County loses one of her best and most public spirited men."

Chapter 4 Cathey's Mill

1. Horace Kephart, *Our Southern Highlanders: A Narrative of Adventure in the Southern Appalachians and a Study of Life among the Mountaineers* (New York: McMillan, 1913), p. 366.

2. Colton, *Legends, Tales and History of Cold Mountain, Book 4,* p. 78.

3. E. H. (Dred) Blaylock was listed as a thirty-three-year old mechanic in the U.S. census of 1850 for Haywood County, North Carolina. In June 1861, at the age of forty-four years, he enlisted in Company F of the 25th Regiment North Carolina Infantry Troops. These facts indicate that he would have been about twenty-eight years old in the mid-1840s when the Cathey mill is thought to have been built.

Chapter 5 A Drove to Market

1. Wm Hartgrove's Book.

2. Blackmun, *Western North Carolina,* pp. 109–14 and pp. 215–20. Details of the turnpike route, livestock droves, and drove stations were gleaned from this interesting work.

3. Blackmun, *Western North Carolina,* p. 353.

4. Arthur, *Western North Carolina,* p. 237.

5. Wm H. Hartgrove's Book.

6. Arthur, *Western North Carolina,* pp. 239–40.

7. Douglas Swain, ed., *Cabins and Castles: The History and Architecture of Buncombe County, North Carolina* (Asheville, N.C.: Bright Mountain Books, 1981); Talmage Powell, "Asheville: An Historical Sketch," p. 38.

Chapter 7 Jim Hargrove's Western Adventure

1. Ida Reid and Mary Hargrove, "Pine[y] Grove Church: Seventy Years Ago and Now—1948," Nov. 1948. This handwritten three-page document, a copy of which is in the author's possession, is signed, "Nov 1948, Written by Ida Reid and Mary Hargrove." It is an interesting, informative, and informal history of the Piney Grove

Church located in Stamey Cove. Mary Hargrove was married to Hack Hargrove's son, Joseph, and was sister to Margaret (Maggie), Jim Hargrove's wife.

2. Evelyn Colton, "Mills, Milling, and Millers," in *Legends, Tales & History of Cold Mountain: A Pigeon Valley Heritage Collection, Book 4*, 2008. Colton's research indicates that the original mill, owned and operated by Colonel Joseph Cathey, was built by Dred Blaylock sometime in the 1840s. It burned in 1869 just after the Civil War and was subsequently rebuilt. After Colonel Cathey's death in 1874 the mill continued to operate for years under the ownership of his son-in-law, Captain James Allen Blaylock, and later Jonathan Plott.

3. This tale was repeated numerous times to the author by Jim Hargrove's daughters, Jimmie Hargrove Jones and Nannie Hargrove Smathers.

4. Genealogy information on the Haywood County Hargroves' trek to Montana was researched and recorded by Tony C. Jones.

5. Information on hard-rock mining was gleaned from Robert Wallace's *The Miners* (Alexandria, Va.: Time-Life Books, 1976), and various Web sites, including www.frontiertrails.com/oldwest/mining.html.

6. Information on Beatty, Nevada, and the Bullfrog Mining District was taken from various Web sites, including www.beattynevada.org and www.beattymuseum.com.

7. Certificates of claim locations from Bullfrog Mining District found in "Mining Locations," Book 38, p. 470; Book 40, pp. 634, 635; and Book 42, p. 364. Copies of these hand-written documents were given to the author by Bill Holbrook.

8. Letter, Apr. 23, 1909, from J. B. Hargrove, Flourine, Nev., to Dr. T. A. Hargrove, Canton, N.C., collection of Bill Holbrook, Bethel, N.C.

9. Information on Skidoo and the story of Hootch Simpson's hanging is found at various Web sites, including the National Park Service site at http://www.nps.gov/archive/deva/Skidoo.htm.

10. This single ledger sheet, given to the author by Nannie Hargrove Smathers, has penciled entries and is stamped "Paid – March 18, 1913."

11. All Eagles and Odd Fellows receipts and records referred to in this story were given to the author by Nannie Hargrove Smathers.

12. Membership booklet for Western Federation of Miners has stamps pasted in it for the months of July 1910 through January 1912. The small red booklet was given to the author by Nannie Hargrove Smathers.

13. These old bank records were given to the author by Nannie Hargrove Smathers.

14. The three letters written to James Hargrove from his miner friends and from which so much has been deduced or presumed were given to the author by Nannie Hargrove Smathers.

15. Wallace, *The Miners*, p. 94.

Chapter 8 The Old Canton Water Gap

1. Arthur, *Western North Carolina* pp. 55, 379.

2. Allen, *Annals of Haywood County.* The notion of a "water gap" near Canton and the inspiration to write about it came from reading part 1, pp. 11–22 of Allen's book.

3. *New Scientist* magazine states that the species *homo sapiens* appeared on the scene approximately 195,000 years ago. See John Pickrell, "Timeline: Human Evolution," at the magazine's Web site, www.newscientist.com/channel/being-human/human-evolution/dn9989-timeline-human-evolution.html, accessed 2007.

4. See "Geologic Provinces of the United States: Appalachian Highland Province" at http://geomaps.wr.usps.gov/parks/province/appalach.html. See also online article by Kempton H. Roll, "The Southern Appalachian Mountains: How They Got Where They Are," www.main.nc.us/sams/blueridge.html, accessed 2007.

The geologic time scale is taken from http://en.wikipedia.org/wiki/Geologic_time_scale, accessed 2007.

Chapter 10 Summer: A Time for Growing

1. William J. Weber, *Rugged Hills, Gentle Folk: My Friends and Neighbors in the Big Pine Valley* (Greendale, Wisc.: Country Books/Reiman Publications, 1995), pp. 66, 67.

2. Alice Hawkins Haynes, *Haywood Home: Memories of a Mountain Woman*, (Tallahassee, Fla.: Rose Printing Company, 1991), pp. 46–49 and Medford, *Early History*, pp. 76, 77.

3. Haynes, *Haywood Home*, pp. 48.

Chapter 11 REMINISCENCES OF A CANTON BOY

1. Camille Wells, *Canton: The Architecture of Our Home Town*, Mountaineer Graphics, 1985, p. 26: This source states that in 1894 officials from Pigeon River village ordered an iron truss bridge from the Wrought Iron Bridge Company in Canton, Ohio, to span the Pigeon River. After the bridge was completed a local citizen, Cash I. Mingus, is credited with the suggestion to change the name of the small village to "Canton." It is supposed that he came up with the idea from the manufacturer's name plate riveted to the bridge. His idea caught on and the name of "Canton" was made official in 1895.

Chapter 13 PLUMB PROUD OF MY MOUNTAIN DIALECT

1. Blackmun, *Western North Carolina*. The first several chapters of this interesting work provide details of the settlement of western North Carolina.

2. Blackmun, *Western North Carolina*, pp. 109–14 and 215–20.

3. Medford, *Middle History*. The author provides an account of Haywood County's history following the Civil War, describing the entry of the railroad into the region and the subsequent growth of its industry and economy.

4. Horace Kephart, *Our Southern Highlanders*, 1913, chapter 16 and p. 353 in particular.

5. Many of these listed expressions, idioms, and words are taken from Horace Kephart's *Our Southern Highlanders*, first published in 1913. Others are drawn from the author's own vocabulary and were acquired from living among the mountain folk of Haywood County.

Sources

Books

Allen, W. C. *The Annals of Haywood County North Carolina, Historical, Sociological, Biographical, and Genealogical.* 1935; repr. Spartanburg, S.C.: Reprint Company, 1977.

Arthur, John Preston. *Western North Carolina: A History (from 1730 to 1913).* Asheville, N.C.: Edward Buncombe Chapter of the Daughters of the American Revolution of Asheville, North Carolina, 1914 repr. Johnson City, Tenn.: Overmountain Press, 1996.

Barney, William L. *The Making of a Confederate: Walter Lenoir's Civil War.* Oxford and New York: Oxford University Press, 2008.

Blackmun, Ora. *Western North Carolina: Its Mountains and Its People to 1880.* Boone, N.C.: Appalachian Consortium Press, 1977.

Haynes, Alice Hawkins. *Haywood Home: Memories of a Mountain Woman.* Tallahassee, Fla.: Rose Printing Company, 1991.

Jones, Carroll C. *The 25th North Carolina Troops in the Civil War: History and Roster of a Mountain-Bred Regiment.* Jefferson, N.C.: McFarland, 2009.

Kephart, Horace. *Our Southern Highlanders: A Narrative of Adventure in the Southern Appalachians and a Study of Life among the Mountaineers.* New York: McMillan, 1913.

Medford, W. Clark. *The Early History of Haywood County.* Asheville, N.C.: Miller Printing Co., 1961.

———. *The Middle History of Haywood County.* Asheville, N.C.: Miller Printing Co., 1968.

Swaim, Douglas, ed. *Cabins and Castles: The History and Architecture of Buncombe County, North Carolina.* Asheville, N.C.: Bright Mountain Books, 1981; Talmage Powell, "Asheville: An Historical Sketch," p. 38.

Wallace, Robert. *The Miners.* Alexandria, Va.: Time-Life Books, 1976.

Weber, William J. *Rugged Hills, Gentle Folk: My Friends and Neighbors in the Big Pine Valley.* Greendale, Wisc.: Country Books/Reiman Publications, 1995.

Wells, Camille. *Canton: The Architecture of Our Home Town.* Waynesville, N.C.: Mountaineer Graphics, 1985.

Journals, Magazines, and Other Sources

Colton, Evelyn M. *Legends, Tales, and History of Cold Mountain: A Pigeon Valley Heritage Collection, Book 4.* Waynesville, N.C.: Richard L. Coltman, 2008.

Erwin, Rev. Thomas. *Life Sketches of Thomas Erwin*. Unpublished family history in personal collection of Carroll Jones, c. 1970s.

Hargrove, W. H. *Diary and Reminiscences of W. H. Hargrove.* Sweetwater, Tex.: privately printed by Hattie Rue and Dale Campbell, 1938.

Hargrove, W. H. "Wm H. Hartgrove's Book." Unpublished notebook/journal in possession of Carroll Jones.

Haywood County, N.C. Commissioners' Court records.

Haywood County Schoolin': A Rich Heritage. [n.p.]: Haywood County Schools History Book Committee, c. 1991.

Iglesias, Loralee Kendall. "Colonel Joseph Cathey of Haywood County, North Carolina: Nineteenth Century Merchant, Entrepreneur, and Community Leader." Unpublished thesis submitted Nov. 21, 2003, University of North Carolina at Asheville.

Genealogy records of the Hargrove and Cathey families of Haywood County, North Carolina. Compiled by Albert C. (Tony) Jones; collection of Carroll Jones.

Reid, Ida, and Mary Hargrove. "Pine[y] Grove Church: Seventy Years Ago and Now—1948." [n.p.], Nov. 1948.

Newspapers

Canton (N.C.) Vindicator. Miscellaneous 1908 and 1909 newspaper publications on microfilm, North Carolina State Archives and Records, Raleigh, N.C.

The Mountaineer (Waynesville, N.C.). Bicentennial Edition, July 1976.

Ross, Kathy. "Haywood History, 1809–Civil War." Supplement to *The Mountaineer.* Waynesville, N.C.: Mountaineer Publishing Co., c. 2005.

Web sites

www.frontiertrails.com/oldwest/mining.html.

www.beattynevada.org and www.beattymuseum.com.

www.nps.gov/archive/deva/Skidoo.htm.

Pickrell, John. "Timeline: Human Evolution." www.newscientist.com/channel/being-human/human-evolution/dn9989-timeline-human-evolution.html.

"Geologic Provinces of the United States: Appalachian Highland Province," http://geomaps.wr.usps.gov/parks/province/appalach.html.

Roll, Kempton H. "The Southern Appalachian Mountains: How They Got Where They Are." www.main.nc.us/sams/blueridge.html.

Special Collections

Lenoir Family Papers. Southern Historical Collection, Wilson Library, University of North Carolina at Chapel Hill.

Tennent, Gaillard. "The Indian Path in Buncombe County" map [ind002], D. H. Ramsey Library, Special Collections, University of North Carolina at Asheville. Originally published Asheville, N.C.: Stephens Press, n.d. [after 1950?].

Acknowledgments

THE ASSORTED STORIES COMPILED IN THIS WORK over a period of two or three years represent the first serious literary efforts in my writing career. Now that I think about it, I believe it was the discovery of that obituary clipping of my great-grandfather Hack that first incited me to dig up the past and sketch his amazing life story for family members to enjoy. Kind words of praise and encouragement from the few relatives and friends who I allowed to read about Hack spurred me to continue writing. The accounts contained herein are the fruits that quickly followed. To all those who read early drafts of these stories and gave me feedback in one form or another I want to express my gratitude, especially Edie Hutchins Burnette, who generously provided the foreword to this work. Thank you so much, everyone, for your time, your honesty, your shared thoughts, and, most of all, your friendship.

Of course this anthology comprises more than just a compilation of historical writings. Woven through a goodly portion of the contents are my personal memories and visions of how things used to be, or how I imagine they were. For the bountiful memories I have accumulated, especially during my growing-up years in Canton, I have many folks to credit. Certainly my parents and brother, to whom this book is dedicated, were responsible for most of them. However, I would also like to generally acknowledge the following donors who made significant contributions to my memory bank: my former schoolteachers and classmates, my ball coaches and teammates, the citizens of Canton, our Pearl Street neighbors, family friends, and close Hargrove relations.

One of the closest Hargrove relatives and a person who patiently and lovingly fed the inquisitive mind of her young towheaded nephew was Aunt Nannie Hargrove Smathers. The keeper of Hargrove and Pigeon Valley lore, Nannie was always anxious to share her intelligence with us young'uns, surely hoping that it might somehow be retained for yet another generation. I am truly indebted to this warm, beautiful, and generous woman for all the love, family documents and heirlooms, and fond memories she gave me over the years.

Additionally, this book is filled with artwork, paintings, maps, and photographs to illustrate the stories. I am grateful to all those who have given permissions and loaned paintings, documents, and photographs to be used in such a manner:

Paintings and illustrations from various eras provide the reader a picture of Western North Carolina, then and now. Nineteenth-century engravings such as those in *Harper's New Monthly Magazine* and Wilbur G. Zeigler and Ben S. Grosscup's *The Heart of the Alleghanies* are now in the public domain. Paintings by Elizabeth Cramer McClure from Ora Blackmun's *Western North Carolina, Its Mountains and Its People to 1880* (Boone, N.C.: Appalachian Consortium Press, 1977) are used by permission of the publisher.

Nettie Vance Penland's painting "The Cathey Mill," reproduced from Evelyn Coltman's *Legends, Tales & History of Cold Mountain,* books 3 and 4, is in the collection of Eula Rigdon and is used by permission.

Digital images of Jo Ridge Kelly's watercolor paintings "Gift from Heaven" and "Old Home Place" have been generously provided by the artist and are used by permission.

Various images come from the online photographic collections of the Library of Congress, including the George Grantham

Bain Collection (#LC-USZ62-78069) and the Farm Security Administration/Office of War Information Collection (#LC-USF34-055634-D, #LC-USG34-000365-D).

Historical photographs and documents reproduced herein survive among archives and collections of family members and friends, thanks to our predecessors' care in preserving them and passing them along. In addition to materials in my possession, I borrowed from the private collections made available by Charles Cathey, Bill and Earlene Holbrook, and the Canton Area Historical Museum.

Barbara Brannon of Winoca Press painstakingly edited my stories and offered many helpful suggestions to improve the organization and construction of the book. Many thanks, also, go to her staff, especially Steven Hendricks for his preparation work on the images and Betty Brannon for the final proofing.

Last, I want to recognize my closest and best friend, whose companionship I have now enjoyed for more than a quarter of a century: Maria, my wife. Her patience seems to be interminable, and the support that she offers is always steady and strong. It is she who puts up with my periods of seclusion when writing, and it is she who always lends an ear when asked "Maria, how do you think this sounds?" More often than not there are some quirks or occurrences of tangled prose that must be cleaned up, and she is a master at pointing them out. For all of this and much more, I am not only grateful but am forever devoted to her.

Index Illustrations indicated by italics

This book was composed in the Warnock Pro
and Birch fonts in Adobe InDesign CS4 on
the Macintosh computer.

LaVergne, TN USA
02 October 2009
159723LV00003B/3/P